T0305927

# Entrepreneurship for Rural Start-ups

Entrepreneurs who start out with no network, no money, no market and scarce resources find a big contrast between what they read in books and the success stories from the Valley and their reality, especially first-timers. Most entrepreneurial books focus on the Business Canvas Model, simplifying the process of building a start-up. Many entrepreneurs who have no previous business experience embrace quick and lean methods without the foundations needed to build solid value proposals.

This book stands out because it deals with entrepreneurship in environments far removed from large cities with fewer infrastructures, connections and resources but which also need companies that provide services to citizens and society. This book focuses on the basics, treating each part of the business canvas as a discipline itself that must be mastered. The book illustrates key lessons learned and offers guidance on essential topics for new venture success in mainstream markets. It expands critical lessons learned and points of guidance across several key topics for new venture creation. Noteworthy is the role of context, financial understanding, building business development skills and start-up communications.

*Entrepreneurship for Rural Start-ups* will be of interest to students, academics and researchers in the field of entrepreneurship, and will be of use to individuals looking to start a local business to take advantage of the rural environment and the possibilities it offers.

**Gloria Jiménez-Marín** is Professor in the Audiovisual Communication and Advertising Department at the University of Seville, Spain.

**Alejandro López Rodríguez** is an entrepreneur and CEO of 360° Heritage, Spain.

**Miguel Torres García** is Director of Knowledge Transfer and Entrepreneurship at the University of Seville, Spain.

**José Guadix Martín** is Professor of Business Organization and Vice-Rector of Technology Transfer at the University of Seville, Spain.

# Routledge Focus on Business and Management

The fields of business and management have grown exponentially as areas of research and education. This growth presents challenges for readers trying to keep up with the latest important insights. *Routledge Focus on Business and Management* presents small books on big topics and how they intersect with the world of business research.

Individually, each title in the series provides coverage of a key academic topic, whilst collectively, the series forms a comprehensive collection across the business disciplines.

**Entrepreneurship and Work in the Gig Economy**
The Case of the Western Balkans
*Mirjana Radović-Marković, Borislav Đukanović, Dušan Marković and Arsen Dragojević*

**Innovation Research in Technology and Engineering Management**
A Philosophical Approach
*Marc J. de Vries*

**Rethinking Organizational Culture**
Redeeming Culture through Stories
*David Collins*

**Management in the Non-Profit Sector**
A Necessary Balance between Values, Responsibility and Accountability
*Renato Civitillo*

For more information about this series, please visit: www.routledge.com/ Routledge-Focus-on-Business-and-Management/book-series/FBM

# Entrepreneurship for Rural Start-ups

Lessons and Guidance for New Venture Creation

**Edited by Gloria Jiménez-Marín,
Alejandro López Rodríguez,
Miguel Torres García and
José Guadix Martín**

 Routledge
Taylor & Francis Group

NEW YORK AND LONDON

First published 2021
by Routledge
52 Vanderbilt Avenue, New York, NY 10017

and by Routledge
2 Park Square, Milton Park, Abingdon, Oxon, OX14 4RN

*Routledge is an imprint of the Taylor & Francis Group, an informa business*

*Library of Congress Cataloging-in-Publication Data*
Names: Jiménez-Marín, Gloria, 1980– editor.
Title: Entrepreneurship for rural start-ups : lessons and guidance
   for new venture creation / edited by Gloria Jiménez-Marín,
   Alejandro López Rodríguez, Miguel Torres García, José Guadix
   Martín.
Description: New York, NY : Routledge, 2021. | Series: Routledge
   focus on business and management | Includes bibliographical
   references and index.
Identifiers: LCCN 2020046666 (print) | LCCN 2020046667 (ebook) |
   ISBN 9780367522667 (hbk) | ISBN 9781003057239 (ebk)
Subjects: LCSH: Entrepreneurship. | New business enterprises. |
   Rural industries.
Classification: LCC HB615 .E77835 2021 (print) | LCC HB615 (ebook) |
   DDC 658.1/1—dc23
LC record available at https://lccn.loc.gov/2020046666
LC ebook record available at https://lccn.loc.gov/2020046667

ISBN: 978-0-367-52266-7 (hbk)
ISBN: 978-1-003-05723-9 (ebk)

Typeset in Times New Roman
by Apex CoVantage, LLC

Dedicated to all the brave people who find
in entrepreneurship a way of life.

Dedicated to our main entrepreneurial projects
in life: Andrea, Claudia, Miguel and Blanca.

# Contents

*Forewords*                                                                      ix
*Acknowledgements*                                                               xv


**PART I**
**Basic Principles for Successful Rural Entrepreneurship**                        1

1 **First Steps: Understanding the Start-Ups Ecosystem**                          3
  IGNACIO MORALES CONDE, JOSÉ L. CÓRDOBA LEIVA
  AND SUSAN GIESECKE

2 **Where Is the Money? Funding and Finances**                                    9
  FÉLIX JIMÉNEZ-NAHARRO, MARÍA DEL MAR
  GONZÁLEZ-ZAMORA AND TOM HORSEY

3 **How Do I Sell It? Marketing and Communication**
  **Fundamentals**                                                               16
  GLORIA JIMÉNEZ-MARÍN AND MARTA DOMÍNGUEZ DE LA
  CONCHA-CASTAÑEDA

4 **Business Development and Day-to-Day Operations**                             24
  RODRIGO ELÍAS ZAMBRANO AND JAVIER DOMINGO MORALES

5 **Assembling a Tech Team**                                                     30
  EMILIO SOLÍS BUENO AND ÁLVARO PAREJA DOMÍNGUEZ

6 **Legal Tips for Newcomers**                                                   39
  VÍCTOR LÓPEZ PÉREZ AND RICARDO SAN MARTÍN

7 **Dealing (and Working) With Large Companies**                                 43
  ÓSCAR CARRERAS AND PATRICIA HERNANZ FALCÓN

**PART II**
**Entrepreneurship With Rural Start-Ups**                    49

8   **Spain**                                                51
    COORDINATOR: PATRICIA LÓPEZ TRABAJO

    *360° Heritage  51*
    *Imperfectus  53*
    *Sunjob  55*
    *MYHIXEL  56*
    *BrioAgro Tech  58*
    *PigCHAMP  59*
    *Kharty  60*
    *Alén Space  62*

9   **USA**                                                  65
    COORDINATOR: SUSAN GIESECKE

    *Zero Grocery  65*

10  **Portugal**                                             67
    COORDINATOR: PEDRO ALVARO PEREIRA CORREIA

    *Connecting Software  67*
    *Press Power  68*

11  **Latin America (Peru and Brazil)**                      70
    COORDINATOR: PATRICIA M. FARIAS COELHO

    *Agros  70*
    *Ticsart  71*
    *Evobooks  73*

12  **United Kingdom**                                       75
    COORDINATOR: IRENE GARCÍA MEDINA

    *Beira  75*
    *Yellow Bird Digital  76*

    *About the Contributors*                                 78
    *Index*                                                  83

# Forewords

*Belén Márquez*

**Belén Márquez**
*Associate Creative Director/Art Director at WhatsApp
(Facebook Inc.) CA, USA*

## The Value to Entrepreneur in a Rural and Global World

In 2003, Mark Zuckerberg created a virtual directory with names and photographs of all the students at his university—Harvard. He was setting the stage for what would later become a multi-billion-dollar business on which millions of global organizations, small businesses, entrepreneurs and other sites would depend. Zuckerberg built a platform for communities large and small to flourish, while also creating platforms for each of us to be photographers, videographers, writers, innovators and leaders. Although Facebook's original intent was a directory of faces and short profiles to introduce and make the world of higher education smaller and easier to get to know people, the truth is that in 2020 it is a social network used in more than 120 languages and with a presence in countries such as India, Argentina, Brazil, Indonesia and the Philippines. In 2014, when Facebook acquired WhatsApp for $16B, some thought it was crazy. Facebook was chasing user growth. Today, in 2020, as most mobile phones are IP-based and Internet access is more widely available globally, WhatsApp is the leader in instant messaging for much of the world, touting 2 billion daily users.

And that's where I come in. I was born in 1989 in an Extremaduran village of about 8,000 residents in Spain. Nobody understands the rural concept better than I do, the core of this book you have in your hands. Entrepreneurship was created in rural areas all over the world and has evolved over thousands of years. In rural towns, you maximize resources and individuals to grow and evolve the people, resources and overall small economy. We all wear many hats and by pure circumstance are creative in how we solve problems. I spent my most formative years in a village watching my family grow their textile business and eventually decided to move to the city to get an education. I learned as much as I could from people of all different backgrounds and experiences. I went through several advertising agencies, working as a Creative/Art Director on projects for brands such as Coca-Cola, Chase, American Express, Sperry and even anti-suicide initiatives for the JED Foundation and AD Council—still learning, of course. I have lived in several cities: Seville, Madrid, New York, London, Prague, San Francisco. In each city, in each country and in each job, I have found different ways to approach social problems with brave, bold and imaginative solutions regardless of the resources and funding at hand.

In my career, I have had the opportunity to work on incredible and satisfying projects, but the one I am most proud of is The Refugee Nation, where, together with a group of colleagues and refugees, we independently created a flag and an anthem to represent and support more than 65 million displaced people around the world. Working on this project made me realize the responsibility we have as creatives not only to solve business problems, but also to use our skills and creativity to give voices to the voiceless, help people share their stories and ultimately shed light on global issues to drive social change. It's the best and the biggest *entrepreneurial* project that I have ever done.

A year ago, I signed up with WhatsApp, from Facebook. What this app brings to us is a hyper-connected global world where people can be their true selves and experience real relationships. We no longer understand the world without WhatsApp. The digital natives, in fact, do not conceive the pre–WhatsApp era. WhatsApp has revolutionized communications, the way we connect to people in different parts of the planet and, in situations such as those experienced as a result of the global pandemic caused by Covid-19, this app has allowed us to see and interact with each other intimately, from 8,000 km away. Living abroad, away from my family for more than 5 years, WhatsApp has become my lifeline. It is the only way to keep in touch with family and friends without spending hundreds of euros a month. This helped me understand what the brand offers and stands for, in turn helping me to create communication for it with true human insights. I believe that any kind of innovation should always be welcome, especially if it helps the human being to develop. And even more so if it manages to link people together and to make everyone's life easier regardless of where they live. Today entrepreneurship can be undertaken from anywhere in the world. The old barriers to entrepreneurship in the rural world, thanks to technologies, are minimized, become diffuse and, in many cases, are erased.

To all entrepreneurs. From any point on this planet. The world needs you to be an entrepreneur.

**José Guadix Martín, PhD**
*Technological Transfer Vice-Rector,*
*University of Seville*

Human beings have always had the ability to improve and overcome difficult moments in their thousands of years of existence. The circumstances we live in now are no different. Entrepreneurs, with the ability to do new things and who know how to adapt to the new environment, have the perfect opportunity to act. Many activities, professions and businesses will change, some will even disappear, as has always happened in history, so these niches will have to be occupied by new actors, with an attitude of change.

Excellent professionals have joined together in this book to try to transfer their knowledge and experience in order to facilitate people who wish to start it up in a rural environment. Actually, in the world of entrepreneurship we have focused too much on an urban environment, or even on big cities, forgetting or leaving aside the other group of areas and people, many of them 'Quijotes'. These people from their town or village, however, have decided to contribute their grain of sand to allow their family or community to live differently, adding value with ideas based on tradition, organic or small-scale crops, artisanal ways of producing or making known the experiences of living in nature.

This work has been divided into two blocks, one more theoretical that will serve as a specific consultation on the specific need that each of us may have and another more practical with real cases from Europe, North America and South America, which are reflected in different start-ups that emerged in recent years, which can serve as inspiration or accompaniment to those that are to come.

You can always innovate, improve existing processes and products and even dare to bring new ones to market. But in exceptional circumstances, when the world changes and society has to adapt to a new order, these people are more necessary than ever, holding in their hands the possibility of influencing society in the next few hundred years. We need all of you who can propose revolutionary ideas in agriculture, animal husbandry, production or use of waste. All this without forgetting the ethics of society, which all of us have in mind while acting to improve the world in which we live.

**Miguel Arias**
*Telefonica, Global Entrepreneurship Director*

Since the beginning of our *Open Future* initiative at Telefonica, working together with public and private partners, we had a clear vision around the concept of *think global, act local* so that we could empower entrepreneurs to succeed in many nonmainstream locations around our footprint from Spain to the UK or LATAM.

I feel this vision is even more relevant nowadays with the global Covid-19 pandemic abruptly changing behavioural patterns and defining a new future, with hard challenges but also full of opportunities ahead.

The massive digitalization we have experienced over the last months and the extensive expansion of our virtual selves throughout the lockdown has made more apparent than ever how relevant strong connectivity is in our modern society.

And this statement is much more relevant for rural areas which have been traditionally separated from the digital world. We are committed as a company to support the access to broadband connectivity with an extensive deployment of infrastructure over the last years, which will continue in the future. We feel that we are not just enabling the transfer of data but actually the connection of lives.

We have often heard that Silicon Valley is not just a place but an attitude and in this 'new normal' stage where remote work is here to stay, we will experience how talent can flourish from all around the world, how ideas can be executed and companies built all around the globe and how many skilled professionals will choose high quality of life in rural areas instead of lengthy commutes and pollution.

This book showcases great rural entrepreneurs who are innovating in various sectors with a global mindset, creating high value in their home regions and paving the path for a more sustainable future where disruption happens everywhere. They are the role models for many other innovators to come and we can learn a ton through their experiences, successes and, why not, failures.

The future looks bright for entrepreneurs in this volatile world and location is no longer a limiting factor!

**Francisco Polo**
*High Commissioner for Spain Entrepreneurial Nation*

## Advancing Towards the Entrepreneurial Society

When we think of the greatest inventions in the history of humanity, it is easy to remember the most universal or the closest to our hearts. Everyday objects like the personal computer, the cell phone or the radio come quickly to our minds. However, it is difficult to find out how they came to be. Mainly because—most of the time—the story we get told is not the whole story. This is, for example, the case of the eBook.

I am rather sure you have never heard about Ángela Ruiz Robles (1895–1975), a pioneer who fell into oblivion for many years, but to whom we owe much. Ángela was a Spanish teacher who pioneered a technology that made possible what today is a very well-known everyday object: the eBook. From a remote, quaint village in rural Spain, she created the first prototype of the device and patented it in 1949 (patent #190,968) under the description of a 'mechanical, electrical and air pressure procedure for reading books'.

The story of this innovator is directly connected to the essence of this book because it conveys one basic truth: innovative solutions to universal problems can be found anywhere. Just like Ángela imagined a way to free her students from the burden of carrying so many books on their backs, these pages are filled with stories of entrepreneurs who have brilliant ideas and who are carrying out innovative projects and articulating change even in the most remote and unexpected corners of the world. Their stories deserve to be told.

We must not let our inventors and promoters of the 21st century, our future entrepreneurs, walk alone. We must build a philosophy of entrepreneurship where creators feel safe founding businesses, innovating and having ideas. And in that sense, all governments must create more opportunities so that anyone with a great idea—regardless of gender, age, income or place of origin or residence—can have the chance to develop it.

In order to generate these opportunities, public administrations and private organizations must pursue a plan aimed at building an economic and social model that promotes the leverage of productivity. A good model for this is the pyramid of entrepreneurship, a model with three interconnected levels: at the top of this pyramid we have innovation-based entrepreneurship; in the middle, the largest industries and corporations of each country; and at the base of the pyramid we find the citizens, each and every one of them, because to ensure the well-being of all members of our society, our people and their interests must be the bedrock of our work.

Working with a model that, at its core, takes inclusive development policies into account is fundamental. In current societies there are growing inequalities which demand us to work resolutely to eliminate them. I am referring to the great gaps of our time, such as the gender gap, the socioeconomic gap, the generational gap and the territorial gap. The four of them exemplify different dimensions of inequality that are also manifested in the innovation ecosystem itself.

Rural entrepreneurs—the core of this book—face inequalities and disadvantages from the get-go and every day through the development of their projects. Promoting initiatives that support entrepreneurs, regardless of where they have decided to live or start up, weaving an innovative entrepreneurial network that expands different geographical areas and building entrepreneurial centres everywhere are some of the actions that will help us achieve this entrepreneurial and innovative atmosphere and, as a consequence, prosperity in our societies.

We are facing a time of accelerated changes, so now more than ever we must bet on great people, on great ideas. We must move forward together by creating opportunities and joining forces to lay the foundations for a more just society. This is an arduous task, but we are prepared for it.

**Sam Brocal**
*Media Interactiva CEO*

## A World Without Borders for Entrepreneurs

Many people are surprised to learn that a world-leading organization in technology and education content that has trained almost half a million people worldwide and sells its products across each of the six inhabited continents actually has its headquarters in Tomares, a little town near Seville, Spain. Equally surprising is that through *MeasureUp*, the organization has become an official provider of practice tests for Microsoft and has been able to develop its own innovative online assessment platform, *Pedagoo*. Also eye-catching is the trust that the organization places in local talent, with many of its employees being graduates from the city and, in the rest of the autonomous community, Andalusia's universities.

As *Media Interactiva* CEO, I would like to say that the business group we founded almost 10 years ago has clearly demonstrated that geographical limits have no place in an ever more globalized world. We have proved that it is possible to form part of the technological elite and to be an entrepreneur in an environment with less than 30,000 population.

Our origins go back to the beginning of my professional career dealing with international clients in Ireland. I then reached a turning point in my career and decided to return to Spain to start my own business, to build on the knowledge and experience acquired and make a commitment to giving the region's young talent an opportunity to prove themselves.

Technology helps to connect the world and to consolidate more competitive personal profiles. It allows us to work with international businesses from our local headquarters. And, while it is true that large technology centres are a magnet for talent and business synergies, we believe that today's world knows no borders and that it is possible to entrepreneur in large cities or rural environments without major difficulties.

Wherever there are experienced professionals, wherever there is hard work and a desire for self-improvement and innovation, wherever there is the vocation to provide solutions, there is an opportunity to grow. From Tomares, we work with teams in the United States of America, India and Ukraine for clients the world over. I can think of no better example of a globalized world: a world without borders.

# Acknowledgements

We would like to express our most sincere thanks to the support of the SCET - Sutardja Center of Entrepreneurship & Technology of the University of California Berkeley and the PAIDI 2020 program (Andalusian Plan for Research, Development and Innovation) of the Knowledge Transfer Activities funded by the Ministry of Economy, Knowledge, Business and University of the Andalusian Government. All this is part of the Europe 2020 Strategy and the H2020 programme (Horizon 2020).

# Part I

# Basic Principles for Successful Rural Entrepreneurship

# 1 First Steps

## Understanding the Start-Ups Ecosystem

*Ignacio Morales Conde, José L. Córdoba Leiva and Susan Giesecke*

### Introduction

I once checked a website of a US institute devoted to researching and developing evidence-based programs to help communities grow outside traditional urban corridors that drew my attention. It claimed "Think today. Thrive tomorrow" as a mantra and it was based on the creation of a think tank focused on rural and small-city innovation and entrepreneurship. Is it possible to do that? Yes, it is. And the reason that it works is resulting in more and more founders seeking opportunities outside of established start-up hubs in Madrid, Barcelona, London, Berlin or Paris. In small cities, entrepreneurs can cut their rent and other living expenses in half, which is a big selling point, and they end up finding places with a relative ease of doing business. It is a reality nowadays that start-ups are finding an opportunity to be raised in cities and remote areas and, therefore, new ecosystems arise and appear everywhere.

The financial benefit of deploying a business in a rural area, where living costs and expenses related to business deployment are more assumable, is an important advantage that should not eclipse the difficulty in these locations to find like-minded peers.

Entrepreneurs need people with whom they can discuss and collaborate to overcome all the hazards that arise when a new project is under development.

Rural areas are frequently lacking the profiles (English-speaking developers, international marketing specialists, financial experts and many others) that are behind a start-up's success. It is not a matter of talent, it is more a matter of adapted talent.

Adapted talent, business mentality and a modern work approach are all part of business culture. To develop a start-up in these areas it is important to establish mechanisms to avoid cultural difficulties, or better, to transform them into allies.

In this first chapter we will focus on understanding the foundations that guarantee the success of an environment prone to creating start-ups, especially in rural environments.

## The Ecosystem

Entrepreneurship as a strategic development intervention could accelerate rural development by creating employment potential as well as keep the young generations interested in staying in the community, reducing unnecessary migration to cities. It is also a nice way to give not-so-reputed public universities a chance to foster entrepreneurship among their students and create a run-your-own-business mindset that leads to the constitution of companies, employment and wealth.

Therefore, within the framework of integrated rural development, entrepreneurship is an enabler to improve the quality of life for individuals, families and communities. However, to make this a reality at the ground level, an enabling environment that encourages entrepreneurship is critical.

Initiatives for entrepreneurship development are necessarily linked with policies in infrastructure, education (starting as early as secondary school), soft digital and social skills development, technology adaptation, research, finance and capacity building. This means that programmes started by the local/regional/national government and the private sector in that direction, or a combination of both, must work together to encourage and support rural entrepreneurs.

An efficient public and private collaboration is key to promoting a growing and stable ecosystem. The public sector should provide the tools that cannot be assumed by the private sector, overcoming the classical focus on facilities and targeting new aspects.

The connectivity infrastructure is one of the main requirements that the government must provide, especially considering the importance of remote work and the necessity of establishing strong and even real-time connections with international communities.

On the other hand, promoting capacity building, developing strategies to make the community larger and enhancing collaboration with existing hubs are paramount in order to surpass the main aspects that restrict start-up progression in the rural areas.

Community-based support and an entrepreneurial ecosystem are also critical to the success of new business owners, more so in the case of young entrepreneurs.

But who is the **rural entrepreneur**? This is the key question in this respect. Is it the traditional farmer, or has the **rural** firm also evolved together with the overall economic transition? The European examples show that **rural** entrepreneurship exists, leading to an economy in **rural** areas that is far from being ignorable and that is definitively linked to local development. Away from the large cities and emerging in mid-size population areas, this type of entrepreneurship is becoming popular, so it is even considered a tool that can provide and guarantee the quality of life.

In rural areas, the business model is usually different, especially for later-life entrepreneurs. They may run solopreneur lifestyle enterprises or businesses that grow slow and steady, eventually employing 10 to 50 people (examples can be found in Seville, such as www.zevenet.com, www.lantia.com or www.galgus.com). However, here the standard Silicon Valley playbook doesn't work, meaning basically that there is no focus on how quickly a business idea can be brought to scale nationally and globally; also, there is a lack of a powerful angel investors network and venture capitalists financing projects looking to profit when the company is sold or goes public.

In short, rural businesses face specific challenges that need to be understood, especially when compared to their urban counterparts:

- Small population size and low density
- The geographic scale of operations and the need for cooperation between areas (rural-rural and urban-rural)
- Isolation, remoteness and distance from each other and centres of population, which translates into being far from markets and lack of economy of scale
- Low educational level, lack of talent and scarce skills (also linked to aging population), for example, in basic computer literacy
- Poor basic infrastructure and limited access to basic services, especially sensitive to having enough broadband connection in place
- The need to take the entrepreneur's community with them, so they need to provide value for the community and not only be profit driven; this explains, for example, why there is a higher ratio of social enterprises in rural environments than in urban areas

But rural areas have strong potential to be hubs for innovative businesses and, above all, have unique benefits—often setting up companies in rural areas is more affordable and the cost of living is lower, not to mention the lifestyle that rural environments offer.

The relationship between rural areas and tourism can be an important driver to promote entrepreneurship. Travel is an information intensive industry and many start-ups are developing marketplaces or apps around travel services. Rural travel services demand is on the rise, moved by a more responsible and sustainable approach to travel, making the mix between technology, digitalization and travel a source of opportunities for new projects launched from rural areas.

## The Incubation

For these reasons, incubation of new rural businesses requires a different approach than for businesses that mainly function in urban areas.

However, incubators, accelerators, co-sharing workspaces and similar signs of urban entrepreneurship have been popping up in small towns and cities. Yes, the obstacles to growth are challenging: geographic isolation, a lack of investment capital and, often, unreliable access to digital technology.

Accelerators and incubators are helping start-ups in realizing their business ideas. They create a structured environment and provide a range of integrated services. The methodology used by accelerators and incubators is key to their success: using one-to-one traditional knowledge transfer, they engage the entrepreneurs in networking activities and peer-to-peer learning processes and expose their teams to a lot of visitors and local events. They provide high- quality mentoring, following the businesses very closely for the whole period of their development. Using their networks, they can engage with a great variety of stakeholders including universities and research organizations, investors and funding organizations, potential customers and other service providers. This network ensures the access to knowledge, new ideas, funding and facilities.

How do accelerators and incubators differ in their execution?

- Incubators are normally run for a longer period (e.g., for a year or longer), while accelerators work with businesses for a short and precise period (e.g., for 4–8 months or even shorter).
- Incubators mostly deal with early to late stage start-ups, whereas accelerators tend to focus on a wider range of businesses (mainly early stage start-ups).
- Accelerators have a stricter selection process on who can enter the programme, whereas incubators do not select that strictly.
- Incubators mostly provide shared space, facilities and consultancy services, whereas accelerators may work with more diverse and innovative methods.

Several key features have been identified through analyzing some accelerator examples and their value proposition:

- Accelerators provide short-term business advice (mainly through mentors); however, they often involve follow-up activities after a few months.

- They put into practice a structured methodology and most often involve a smaller number of entrepreneurs and focus on a specific theme of interest (challenges) or industry.
- Learning is a big part of the process. Expect seminars, workshops and mentorship opportunities. While this can cover a huge array of topics relevant to launching a venture, some of the most valuable is often on the legal side, execution of the business model and the practice of pitching.
- Accelerators involve creative and innovative ways of business support, are flexible in approach and aim to generate new creative business ideas.
- It is common to provide networking/commercial contacts, the possibility to attend events and public relations support throughout the acceleration period.
- They may provide small amounts of seed money to support pilots at the preparatory stage, as well as links to investors and other sources of funding to support scaling-up the original business idea.
- One of the common challenges has been to find and select the right entrepreneurs who are open to new ideas and exchange, are willing to invest the time, and so on.
- Most accelerators take their graduates by the hand once they finish their acceleration programme and fully support other commercial/financial milestones that the start-up may be achieving.

How, then, could a small city provide an attractive structure to give support to local entrepreneurs?

1. The community must develop a vision of success along with a project team of entrepreneurs, founders, businesspeople and leaders to keep progress focused on achievement of the vision. The role of programme directors is very decisive at this point.
2. The strategy to achieve success must be accepted by all partners of influence that make up the ecosystem. This climate of success changes the focus to achievement of the vision. Feeling the support of the community fostering the creation of feasible start-ups must be an element of pride to the adjacent society (e.g., promoting the celebration of a Demo day).
3. The elements of incubator support must be identified, marketed in a value proposition and made available to businesses and potential entrepreneurs, either local or those that could be interested in luring projects from other areas.
4. Attract start-ups with more than one founder. This is mandatory to really thrive in an intense, high-pressure environment and with learning organized by the incubator.

5.   Last, but of great importance, the probability of success must consider meritocracy as a social system in which people/teams advance on the basis of their merits (e.g., performance).

We hope these tips help you identify what to expect from a start-up accelerator/ incubator and how to succeed in performing your business idea in a rural environment.

## Websites to consult

– Link to Silicon Valley Playbook: The guidebook for startups.
– European Network for Rural Development.
– IC2 Institute – Texas University.
– Sillicon Valley Center Blog.
– CSR Mandate – Enabling & Sustainability.
– How Startup Accelerators Work by Forbes.
– Rural Entrepreneurs Are Finding Success Away From Big Cities by Forbes.
– INC review: Why More Entrepreneurs Are Moving Away From Major U.S. Startup Hubs.
– New Zealand Institute for Rural Entrepreneurship.
– International Journal of Entrepreneurial Behaviour & Research article: Rural entrepreneurship or entrepreneurship in the rural – between place and space.
– SCORE volunteer mentoring network.

## References

http://nlintheusa.com/silicon-valley-playbook/ [Accessed on 02/09/2020].
https://enrd.ec.europa.eu/sites/enrd/files/s4_rural-businesses-factsheet_bus-accelerators. pdf [Accessed on 02/06/2020].
https://ic2.utexas.edu/ [Accessed on 10/05/2020].
https://siliconvalley.center/blog/learning-the-silicon-valley-playbook [Accessed on 20/08/2020].
www.csrmandate.org/accelerating-rural-development-through-entrepreneurship/ [Accessed on 18/07/2020].
www.forbes.com/sites/alejandrocremades/2019/01/10/how-startup-accelerators-work/#74175c6644cd [Accessed on 17/07/2020].
www.forbes.com/sites/nextavenue/2020/02/14/rural-entrepreneurs-are-finding-success-away-from-big-cities/#68451ba456a1 [Accessed on 12/09/2020].
www.inc.com/emily-canal/why-entrepreneurs-leave-nyc-sf-for-austin-reno-miami. html [Accessed on 22/08/2020].
www.nzire.net/what-is-rural-entrepreneurship/ [Accessed on 11/08/2020].
www.researchgate.net/publication/273486777_Rural_entrepreneurship_or_ entrepreneurship_in_the_rural_-_between_place_and_space    [Accessed    on 28/07/2020].
www.score.org/blog/small-towns-business-incubators [Accessed on 20/08/2020].

# 2 Where Is the Money? Funding and Finances

*Félix Jiménez-Naharro, María del Mar González-Zamora and Tom Horsey*

## Introduction

In recent years, the business world in general and rural enterprises in particular have suffered a series of changes and transformations as a result of the technological revolution[1] that we have undergone and are still undergoing, which has led to the emergence of new risks and, in turn, many opportunities (García-Gallo *et al.*, 2020). Thus, the rural enterprise has gone from a static situation with little relation to the markets, to a situation of continuous change and from a traditional business model to an innovative one. Consequently, it is facing an increase in globalization, a greater need for increased flexibility and a greater dependence on external agents;[2] all this seeking to adapt to the new environment that is still being built (Bankinter Foundation of Innovation, 2018).

These changes affect where and how to get funding, changes that are most evident and important in the field of rural start-ups. Therefore, and in order for the entrepreneur to be able to obtain adequate financing according to the stage of their business and its level of risk, it is necessary to be clear about a series of fundamental aspects that are based, among others, on the following premises: the entrepreneur's objective must be to earn money, the main means of financing is sales, the financing model has changed, intelligent capital is more important than financial capital, and the business plan must be made with a lot of common sense and with few technicalities.

## Economic Aspects to Consider When You Are Going to Entrepreneur

Here, we focus on those fundamental aspects that should always be kept in mind.

### The Best Method of Financing Is Sales

The objective of the entrepreneur must be to earn money, so they must choose the means of financing (their own resources or external resources) that makes them earn more money, that is, the one that brings them more income and less risk (Jiménez-Naharro & de la Torre Gallegos, 2017). The variable that achieves this objective to the greatest extent is sales.

One of the big problems an entrepreneur must solve is SELLING. Many times, financing is not the main problem of the entrepreneur, but it is the excuse to justify failures or not to undertake. One of the challenges that an entrepreneur must cover is to get intelligent capital (not financial) that will bring value through an increase in sales. Sales must be the fundamental financing source and the rest of the funding instruments must be extraordinary and timely; the company must grow through self-financing.

Getting financing at a 'justified' time (we are not selling yet) can become a short-term solution, but a medium-term problem. The time you are not selling is in the Intensive Care Unit (ICU). And if you also incur expenses, the more time passes, the greater the likelihood of failure. Therefore, if your financing does not generate value, that is, it does not serve you to sell, you only prolong your agony: more time to pay expenses and not to sell. The sooner you leave the ICU, the better (Jiménez-Marín *et al.*, 2020).

When financing does NOT create value, it leads to failure and when financing creates value, it increases the probability of success.

For all these reasons, and without wishing to be repetitive, the entrepreneur must dedicate a large part of their efforts to selling, selling, selling—the main source of financing.

### The Perverse Role of Subsidies: Participatory Loans, Their Main Substitute

The entrepreneur must know that *the financing model has changed*. Many rural businesses have been characterized as a sector benefited by subsidies, which have become an artificial mechanism to make projects viable. An important part of rural companies is viable because of subsidies and not because of their sales.

This is a mistake that a rural entrepreneur should avoid, but not despise. That is, if there are subsidies, they should apply for them, but they should not make their business model dependent on them. Rural start-ups must seek other alternatives, such as innovation and differentiation, so that subsidies become an extraordinary means of financing that add value to the business but are not one of its fundamental elements. This will, among other things, make it easier for the entrepreneur to access other alternative means of financing.

In addition, we must not lose sight of the fact that, increasingly, institutions are demanding the requested financing to be returned, so that subsidies are being replaced by participatory loans, which we will refer to later.

## How to Prepare a Document to Apply for Funding

When an entrepreneur needs to apply for funding, they should prepare a document explaining how much and for what purpose they need funding and what they intend to achieve with their business thanks to the requested funding. The information in this document should be obtained from the business plan.

When you are looking for financing you must answer simple but difficult questions, such as: how much will you sell, how much money will you need, what will you invest in, how much will you spend, how will you make me earn money, how much will I be able to earn? Vague, insecure or meaningless answers can lead you to certain failure. Therefore, it is very important to take the time to solve these questions.

This document must tell what you intend to do and what you intend to achieve and it must be easy to read, avoiding excessive technicalities; estimates must be reasonable, made with common sense, and should always be justified.

Although the business is always the same, this document must be written, structured and quantified differently depending on who you are asking for financing, as each agent needs to listen to a different discourse related to the philosophy of their institution. Keep in mind that everyone speaks a different language (Harris, 2019).

Thus, if you seek financing in a traditional financial institution, what you will be asked for are guarantees, looking for lower risk. These institutions usually offer financing to the entrepreneur and never to the project. Therefore, it is the least advisable option.

If you seek financing from a public institution, it may be that the institution will finance the whole business. This being the case, in your document you must justify that you have an innovative business, which will generate sufficient income to be able to meet all the created needs (cover costs, pay investments, pay back partners and return the financing requested), that the requested financing is necessary to achieve this income and that this income does not exceed the needs. Public institutions do not finance 'bouncers', as they are usually businesses that can be very profitable, but also carry a lot of risk, so they are not in their profile. Thus, when you prepare this document, you must be cautious in your estimates and avoid overly optimistic scenarios that will cause you to fall outside the risk profile requested by these institutions.

If public institutions finance Research and Design and Innovation, in the document you have to justify your research very well and show that it is limited to what is requested by the institution. The quantification of the scenarios is important, but somewhat secondary. This must be a much more technical document than the previous one.

In short, public institutions are looking for innovative business models; multidisciplinary, international teams or the capacity for internationalization; with growth potential, but not excessive; that generate employment, creating the value necessary for participants to live and pay back the obtained financing. All this should be reflected in the document to be drawn up.

If the document is aimed at seeking investors, it must be clear that there is a team with the capacity to materialize the project, sales and expected costs, as well as the profitability that the investor can achieve with the project. In this document you must create much more optimistic scenarios with greater growth potential.

## *Funding Instruments for Rural Start-Ups*

The entrepreneur must be trained and informed about the different resources available in their ecosystem, both public and private.

In this way, the entrepreneur must be aware of the resources available in the European Union (European Agricultural Fund for Rural Development, ERDF funds, etc.). The information about them is accessible through the following link: https://europa.eu/european-union/about-eu/funding-grants_es#solicitar-financiaci%C3%B3n.

On the other hand, the public institutions grant subsidies and participative loans, which are announced annually in accordance with the national budgets, a call to which every entrepreneur must be attentive. We reiterate that, increasingly, participatory loans are replacing subsidies. Participatory loans are financial instruments that provide the company with long-term equity without interfering with its management; finance business projects, covering all types of tangible and intangible investments; are loans with low interest rates, several years' grace period and a longer maturity than traditional loans. They can be of two types:

- Convertible equity loans: after a period and at a stipulated price, the loan becomes the capital of the company.
- Non-convertible equity loans: the loan must be repaid.

In the case of Spain, the following resources are particularly noteworthy:

- **CDTI** (Centre for Technological and Industrial Development):[3] provides advice and training in the idea stage to entrepreneurs, finances in the seed phase, start-up and internationalization of the company and is committed to promoting technological small and medium sized enterprises (SMEs). Its most outstanding support initiatives are:

- **NEOTEC Initiative**: Spanish government initiative to support the creation and consolidation of new technology-based companies in Spain
- **NEOTEC Venture Capital**: Spanish programme for investment in venture capital

- **ICO** (Official Credit Institute):[4] finances entrepreneurial and innovative initiatives.
- **ENISA** (National Innovation Company):[5] provides financing to SMEs linked to innovation.

On the other hand, there are one's own, non-required, and mixed means of financing, among which we can highlight:

- **Family, friends and other own funds** are those additional contributions to the capital of the company made by members close to the entrepreneur. In most cases they are aimed at not losing the investment made, instead of gaining significant capital gains, because the investment decision is based more on the knowledge of the entrepreneur than on criteria of profitability of the business project.
- **Business angels** are individual **investors** (generally entrepreneurs, company managers or savers) who, in a private capacity, contribute their capital, their knowledge and management skills or their network of personal contacts to actively participate in the implementation of the business project, help **entrepreneurs** in business management and obtain **medium-term capital gains**.
- **Business angels networks** act as catalysts in two key points: **capital supply** and **demand**. On the one hand, they capture business projects of interest, both from newly created companies and from companies that want to carry out expansion processes. On the other hand, they identify potential business angels who have the capacity and, above all, the expectation to invest in business projects with a high degree of risk.
- **Crowdfunding** represents a collective cooperation, carried out by people who make a network of donations to raise money or other resources. It can also be called collective financing, collective micro-financing or micro-leadership, as defined by the Government of Spain's Ministry of Industry, Trade and Tourism.

- **Collaborative platforms specialized in crowdfunding** put people who have projects in touch with people who are willing to finance them through contributions. According to the Spanish Crowdfunding Association, there are four types of crowdfunding: reward, donation, investment and loan. Increasingly, numerous platforms are emerging that specialize in each type of consideration, which are positioned as financing channels for entrepreneurial projects.
- The **Initial Coin Offering (ICO)** is a form of collective financing in which investors offer crypto-currencies, supported by blockchain technology, in exchange for tokens that may represent a certain 'ownership' of the company or 'right to participate in the profits', or that may have a specific utility within a chain of blocks, either their own or attached to the crypto-currency with which they are purchased.

  ICOs are the revolution in global corporate finance using the power of blockchain technology. ICOs are much more than financing, they are a technology that allows you to develop a project in a more transparent, more global and uncontrolled way.

Once the different financial instruments have been analyzed, the entrepreneur must identify the moment which they are in (how much they are selling and, if they are not selling, when they are going to sell), the risk profile they have and their capacity to face their obligations. The choice of the appropriate financing instrument depends on the identification of these elements.

## Raising Funds

Raising funds for early stage start-ups isn't easy wherever you are. If it wasn't difficult enough for the CEO to keep the day-to-day operations running by being the accountant, main salesperson, team leader, odd job person and receptionist, as well as trying to keep the company on its strategic roadmap, he or she also needs to be selling their vision in a brave attempt to raise funds before the bank decides that enough is enough. To do this anywhere that isn't a main centre for start-up financing, whether that be San Francisco, London, Berlin or Shenzhen, is even more complex. We don't have a secret recipe that can magically fulfil that task for you; however, we can give you at least one basic idea that might hopefully make it a little easier.

As an investor, the first thing that we look at in relation to a founder is how dedicated they are to their project. One of the ways of doing this is quite simply listening to their vision and gauging how much they really believe in it. If something is close to your heart, then there is more likelihood that you will fight tooth and nail for it; if it is something that just amuses you, then you might give up at the first major crisis and, believe me, you will have to get through many crises before succeeding. Another way that we test this is by how much the founders pay themselves in salary. We don't think it a coincidence that some of the most successful companies that we have invested in have had founders that either don't receive a salary for the first couple of years or pay themselves on a pure commission basis. In my first company as an entrepreneur (Tom) I didn't receive a salary from my own company for the first 3 years, so for me it just goes with the terrain. A third way of checking this, of course, which in effect is very similar to the second, is by how much of their own money the founders have invested in the project. If you don't have skin in the game, it is difficult to persuade others to put in theirs and, in our opinion, we should always talk about the four Fs and not just three (i.e., Family, Fools and Friends but also, and most importantly, Founders).

## Notes

1. Internet of Things, artificial intelligence, blockchain, augmented virtual reality, robotics, etc.
2. National and international administrations, financial institutions, customers, suppliers, competitors, investors, etc.
3. www.cdti.es/ [Accessed on 01/09/2020].
4. www.ico.es/web/ico/sobre-ico [Accessed on 01/09/2020].
5. www.enisa.es [Accessed on 01/09/2020].

## References

Bankinter Foundation of Innovation (2018). *Modelos de Negocios Disruptivos*. Retrieved from www.fundacionbankinter.org/documents/20183/156075/Modelos+de+negocio+disruptivos_Resumen/ [Accessed on 19/06/2020].

García-Gallo, M.D.; Jiménez-Naharro, F.; Torres-García, M.; Giesecke, S.; Guadix-Martín, J. (2020). Incorporation of the Intangibles Into the Spanish Start-Ups by Activity Sector and Region. Improving Their Economic Sustainability. *Sustainability*, 12, 4268. https://doi.org/10.3390/su12104268 [Accesed on 01/07/2020].

Harris, T. (2019). *Start-Up: A Practical Guide to Starting and Running a New Business*. Berlin: Springer.

Jiménez-Marín, G.; López Rodríguez, A.; Torres García, M.; Giesecke, S.; Morales Conde, J.I. (2020). *Historias de Emprendimiento Andaluz en Silicon Valley: 9.378 km de Olivares a Berkeley*. Sevilla: McGraw Hill.

Jiménez-Naharro, F.; de la Torre Gallegos, A. (2017). *Valoración de Empresas y Análisis Bursátil*. Madrid: Pirámide.

www.enisa.es/ [Accessed on 22/08/2020].

www.ipyme.org/es-ES/InsFinan/paginas/DetalleInstrumento.aspx?Nombre=Crowdfunding [Accessed on 25/06/2020].

# 3  How Do I Sell It? Marketing and Communication Fundamentals

*Gloria Jiménez-Marín and Marta Domínguez de la Concha-Castañeda*

## Introduction

We would like to make it clear that the important thing is to sell and, above all, to sell from the beginning, even if it is with imperfections, because through the sale and the experience of the first buyers, you learn what your client is really looking for (and paying for).

Knowing the customers is always fundamental, but in the case of start-ups, it is vital, a matter of pure necessity for survival and growth.

Thus, you must answer questions such as: What are your customers looking for? What do they expect from your company? And, above all, for which characteristics of the product/service are they willing to pay? Where do they want to find the product/service?

The basic question is: what value does your product/service bring? This can be specified in:

- What customer need do you satisfy?
- What importance does your client give to this need?
- How much are you willing to pay?
- Where does your differential contribution lie: in the number of users, in the customers willing to pay, in the services you incorporate?
- What feelings does your customer experience with your product/service?

If you answer these questions correctly, you will be able to define your sales objectives and measure the progress, or not, of your commercial actions.

Any start-up or emerging company, rural or urban, must consider its products or services in the context of the competition, adapting it to the needs and/or wishes of potential consumers and buyers. A product that cannot be found on the market is a product that is unlikely to be sold. And, consequently, it will fail. Even more so when we refer to emerging rural companies where, a priori, one might think that the environment is, at least, more complicated.

Success in any project comes from the correct management and planning of the so-called four variables of the marketing mix. These are: Product, Price, Distribution and Communication. But, to begin with, we should be clear about what marketing is.

As it is pointed out by some experts in the subject (Kotler, 2015; Martín, 1993; Santesmases, 1993), we could synthesize the marketing concept as a set of business practices based on a series of principles that seek an increase in purchases, consumption or use of a certain service or product, basically seeking a growth in demand. In other words, and starting from a solid base, marketing tries to make the relationships between customers and companies as beneficial as possible, mainly looking for the profitability of the latter.

## The Variables and Their Importance

In marketing, we speak of the marketing mix as the analysis of the strategies of internal aspects, developed to analyze four basic variables of its activity, being governed by four variables commonly known as the four Ps of the marketing mix, proposed by McCarthy in the first edition of the magazine *Marketing* in the 1960s (Coca Carasila, 2006). In fact, the term marketing mix was disclosed by Borden (1964) but created by Culliton (1948). The most agreed classification is the one offered by McCarthy (1960), (Kotler, 2015) or Vallet & Frasquet (2005). The ingredients that the formula for the marketing mix should have changed, according to the authors who have studied the concept (Vallet & Frasquet, 2005).

Specifically, the variables are:

- Product
- Price
- Place
- Promotion

### *Product*

Product is the variable par excellence of the marketing mix. Without it, the rest of the variables do not develop. It involves the combination of added goods and services that the company offers to the buyer and thanks to which the wishes and/or needs of the buyers are satisfied (Martín, 1993). It is a set of attributes that the consumer considers having a certain good to satisfy their needs or desires. From the point of view of the manufacturer or service provider, the product is a set of elements (physical, chemical, packaging) or services connected in such a way that it offers the user possibilities of use and consumption (Bonta & Farber, 2002). To decide the characteristics that conform the product, you must answer the questions at the beginning of this chapter. In addition, some other questions about the market could be added: which customers want my product? And, What are they like? How much do they buy? Do I want to choose only a segment of the market or more?

If your product is new, you must spend time to get to know your potential customers. You may do interviews or market tests of your product. This information will be fundamental to developing the product. This time with the customers is very important in order to get your product to the market.

Marketing added a second dimension to that traditional definition based on the satisfaction it provides. The first dimension of a product is the one that refers to its characteristics, which are determined in the production process; the second dimension is based on subjective criteria, such as images, ideas, habits and value judgements that the consumer makes about the products (Kotler, 2015).

### Price

This variable is responsible for obtaining the company's income. In order to set the price, the manufacturer must study certain aspects such as the consumer, the market, costs, competition or image, among others, in line with the statements of Díez and Landa (1996).

A first approximation to the price concept would be given as the value, in monetary terms, of a product or service, for which a consumer would be prepared to purchase it. In short, it is the value applied to a good (or service) by the utility perceived by the user and the effort he or she must make, in terms of money, to acquire it. The price can be given, according to the type of good or service, in the form of a fee, canon, toll, salary, commission, wage, contribution or honorarium (Jiménez-Marín, 2016).

A priori, you might think that the only objective of price is to earn as much as possible; however, the price of a product is determined by other issues, from the time the consumer spends to purchase it to the service they receive. This is why, at the same time, it is a matter of achieving maximum customer and company satisfaction, for which both parties must reach an agreement on the price.

The economic and social context demands that a product has a fixed price and this is where the company must put in place all the tools at its disposal to be able to establish the most appropriate price for the market in which it is operating. You have to answer: what importance does your client give to this need? How much are you willing to pay?

In the production or manufacture of products/services, the value of each item is determined from the price of the primary material to which the costs of the successive transformations are added, giving rise to the so-called cost price (CP) to which, subsequently, the profit margin (PM) will be added, giving, as a consequence, the so-called retail price (RP).

Likewise, the question of psychological prices must be considered: some products or services must have a higher price (RP) than the one resulting from the CP+PM formula, as they need a plus in image and prestige to be acquired. This is where intangibles such as the brand, the business group behind the product or even the monopoly/oligopoly situation in that specific market come into play. Other products, on the other hand, need to have a lower RP than the one resulting from the CP+PM formula, also due to external or even internal issues. In both cases the start-up must adjust the final prices, so that, in addition to having an objective formula, it is able to give it the complementary, subjective nuance that makes the final price more appropriate.

## *Place*

We understand place as a commercial distribution, a marketing variable whose objective is to get the products, goods and/or services from the producer or supplier to the buyers or final consumers. It is one of the four variables of the marketing mix that compete in importance with the rest. That is, the combination of the four variables is fundamental, because it would be useless to have a great product at a great price and with phenomenal communication if the buyer or consumer could not access it. However, the truth is that the weight of distribution has not always been the same, due to numerous factors (social, technological, economic or even demographic) which have given rise to the complex commercial system in which we are immersed today. It is important to answer the questions: where do the customers like to buy? How do they want to access the product/service?

Commercial distribution, therefore, brings us closer to the product or service from the manufacturer (supplier) to the consumer (Díez & Landa, 1996).

In this sense, commercial distribution:

- Brings production closer to consumption
- Is of a strategic nature
- Influences all other variables (product, price and communication)

Most of the goods or services that we access are produced far from our area of movement, from our daily work. If we think, for example, of the textile sector, at present most of them may be produced in countries quite far from where we live, such as China, Taiwan, the United States, and so on. If, for example, we think of the agricultural sector, it will be difficult to have production right next to our place of purchase, so we will have to go to fruit shops, supermarkets, shops and so on. Thanks to a number of entities, companies, organizations and people in general, it is possible to move these goods from the place where they are produced to the place where they are consumed. These entities are known as commercial distributors and the different phases through which these products pass are called 'distribution channels'.

Thus, today it is possible to buy through various forms, various channels and in establishments of very different types. And the case of start-ups is no different, even more so when they are developed in or directed to a rural environment. In this sense, we understand distribution channels as the route that the product takes from the manufacturer (or producer) until it reaches the final consumer. This path can depend on the number of intermediaries involved in the process. Thus, we find two types of distribution depending on the intermediaries (Ballou, 2004):

- **Direct distribution**: when there are no intermediaries and, therefore, the sale (rental or service provision) goes directly from the manufacturer to the consumer (or buyer)
- **Indirect distribution**: when there are one or more intermediaries
  In the case of indirect distribution, a further distinction must be made according to the length of the channel. And that's where we can find:

  - **Short indirect channel**: when there is only one intermediary, usually a retailer
  - **Long indirect channel**: when there are two or more intermediaries

### *Promotion*

As has been pointed out, in order to start up and succeed in any project that is initiated, we must have a connection and total understanding between the four variables of the marketing mix. So, there is no point in having a great product if the price is exorbitant, or having a great distribution if the product is, frankly, bad. By this rule of three, communication does nothing on its own. In other words, a good communication campaign can be magical, but let's not get confused—it is not miraculous, either. What is certain is that communication, if well managed, significantly improves the competitiveness of organizations, companies and other entities from different perspectives. And part of the success of a start-up is based on defining how we want to be perceived and, likewise, considering how, indeed, we are perceived. The questions you have to answer are: what feelings does your customer experience with your product/service? Why do they buy? How might you influence these feelings?

When marketing your products or services that your start-up offers to the market, to their (your) customers, or even your company at the corporate level, in general, it is necessary to stand out from the competition. If we start from the basis of the four variables of the marketing mix (product, price, distribution, communication), it is important to know that your company will hardly be able to compete in all variables. You may succeed, but it is much more likely that your company will stand out in one or two of them.

In the market you will find entities that will stand out for the quality of their products, for the price (which does not always have to be low), because it is an easily accessible product (distribution) or for the image and communication that results from its operation.

We cannot factor in the product or service quality; you must be the one who creates it. Pricing and distribution policies must also go hand in hand with your business strategy. But communication, independently of the management of the strategies of the other variables, can be worked on. A lot. And it can give very good results.

It is important to start by saying that there are certain companies that work well despite having poor or almost nonexistent communication. This is not desirable, of course. Well-managed communication will help you reach your target audience more efficiently as well as other sectors of the population of interest, such as suppliers or investors. And the more and better ways you reach your audience, the more beneficial it will be for you.

In fact, the most successful companies are usually those with a great combination of marketing mix strategies. And among them is communication as an intangible asset.

Communication promotes the achievement of objectives and goals previously set by the organization, it contributes to the adaptation to changes in the environment and allows, among other things, publicizing the service or product.

For this reason, most medium and large organizations tend to have specific departments in their organizational charts that manage communication as a marketing variable. And we would almost dare to say that they devote much more effort to communication than, for example, to the variable of price, which does not usually have a specific department. Why? Because communication, far from being an expense, is a profitable investment.

In general, you will have to contemplate several fundamental aspects. It is very important to define and learn to manage your brand in spaces and environments that are increasingly complex and competitive, because your brand is the summary, at a glance, of your product or service. In fact, the consumer identifies products by their brand. In this process of differentiation, 'the consumer recognizes the brands, to which they assign a certain image' (Bonta & Farber, 2002). That is why you must take care to define it and take care of it at a corporate level (the image you have of the company, as an entity) and at a graphic level (the visual image you have of it), because this will contribute to differentiate you from the competition, to position you and to open a space in the mind of your target audience and of society in general. Through properly managed branding you will be able to transmit corporate strategies effectively and efficiently, establishing connections between the expectations of your users or customers (real or potential) and generating value from the economic point of view.

It is important that you think about the media's usefulness and how they can become vehicles for transmitting those central ideas that you have defined for your start-up. The traditional media (press, radio and television, mainly), in addition to emerging technologies such as social networks, CRM (Customer Relationship Management systems) or connected apps, open a huge range of possibilities for your project. Moreover, in recent years, the presence of your start-up on the Internet is crucial, both for the consolidation of the brand image and for building its reputation, and, of course, to make yourself known. Therefore, we recommend that you open an account associated with your start-up on the main social networking platforms: LinkedIn, Instagram, Twitter, Facebook and all those that will arise diachronically over time. In addition to the options for visibility, the presence of your start-up on the Internet will enable two-way communication, that is, to be in direct contact with users, buyers and consumers, suppliers, distributors, shareholders and the general public, and to be able to give them answers and generate impact.

Similarly, strategically managing public relations, communication systems and connection of all audiences (possible and real) by and for the company becomes essential. It is, in fact, one of the bases of large companies: a magnificent relationship with all their publics.

And, in addition, you can try to generate publicity. What is this? It is about generating news of public interest, so that you have media coverage and that the media echo it for free. With this you will get people talking about your start-up, which is a kind of unpaid advertising.

In the same way, investing in advertising in the media (traditional or not) can be a good option. You just must put yourself in the hands of an expert who will tell you where, when and how much to spend (large sums of money do not always imply large media consequences).

In short, and so that you can manage this last variable, communication, as an entrepreneur, we recommend the following:

1.  You must know your audience to the maximum, everything about it: age, socioeconomic level and culture, lifestyle, consumption patterns and so on.
2.  You must position your service or product: generate a positive perception of your company or your product in the minds of your buyers or potential consumers.

3.  You must have a good brand name: naming is essential when positioning your company and establishing it in the relevant market. There are many cases of failure due to the incorrect choice of a name. Think, in addition, of the possibilities of the brand name at an international level, because languages can sometimes generate bad pasts.
4.  Communicate as much as possible with your external audience (potential consumers, real customers, suppliers) and internal audience (mainly workers). You can do this through advertising, but also through other existing communication tools: events, circulars, intranet, CSR (corporate social responsibility), and so on.
5.  You should give your employees as much training as possible, so that they always give the best of themselves and generate the best possible customer service.
6.  You must generate information, content, so that people talk about your company: in the media, at events, on social networks and so on.

In conclusion, you must consider that a satisfied customer will buy into your company and will discuss it with others who may become customers now or in the future. Precisely, sales, current and future, are what guarantee the survival of your company and this, after all, is achieved with the perfect conjunction of the four Ps, always having the customer as the main focus.

## References

Ballou, R.H. (2004). Logística. Administración de la cadena de suministro. Ciudad de México: Pearson.

Bonta, P.; Farber, M. (2002). *199 preguntas sobre Marketing y Publicidad*. Bogotá: Norma.

Borden, N.H. (1964). The Concept of the Marketing Mix. *Journal of Advertising Research*, 4, pp. 5–13.

Coca Carasila, Milton. (2006). El concepto de marketing: pasado y presente. *Perspectivas*, 9(18), julio–diciembre, pp. 41–72.

Culliton, J.W. (1948). *The Management of Marketing Costs*. Boston: Division of Research, Graduate School of Business Administration, Harvard University.

Díez de Castro, E.C.; Landa Bercebal, F.J. (1996). Merchandising: teoría y práctica. Madrid: Pirámide.

Jiménez-Marín, G. (2016). *Merchandising & Retail: Comunicación en el punto de venta*. Sevilla: Advook.

Kotler, Phillip. (2015). *Fundamentos de marketing*. Madrid: Pearson.

Martín Armario, E. (1993). *Marketing*. Madrid: Ariel Economía.

McCarthy, E.J. (1960). *Basic Marketing*. Homewood, IL: Richard D Irwin, Inc.

Santesmases Mestre, M. (1993). *Marketing: conceptos y estrategias*. Madrid: Ediciones Pirámide.

Vallet, T.; Frasquet, M. (2005). Auge y declive del marketing mix. Evolución y debate sobre el concepto. *Revista ESIC Market*, 121(5–8), pp. 142–159.

# 4   Business Development and Day-to-Day Operations

*Rodrigo Elías Zambrano and*
*Javier Domingo Morales*

## Introduction

The business owner, incipient or not, is like the captain of a ship, who must keep his eyes forward at all times to ensure that the course is correct and that the ship does not deviate from its itinerary, checking at all times that the crew is doing its job and, therefore, that everything is in order. With this premise, it is time to warn you that one of the most difficult moments in the life cycle of a start-up occurs when you must begin to consolidate your project, the moment when you stop being an entrepreneur and become a company (Blank, 2013; Blank & Dorf, 2012), because a start-up is no longer a newly created project and becomes a Company, with capital letters. And, therefore, it is time to build and develop the business as such and raise the daily and current operations in the routine business of the company.

If you are not familiar with business language, even if you have been able to set up a start-up (or are thinking of doing so), you should know that the concept of operations is essential for the company to work and be profitable. Operations in a company are those activities that are related to the areas of the company that generate the product or service offered to customers. That is, they are the way of doing things within the company, in such a way that their activities allow them to provide the service or produce the product that is given or delivered to customers to meet their expectations. It is the work of producing the product or service, its quality control, the steps necessary to put the goods on sale, and so on.

## The Operations Goals

The operations have as objectives:

1. **Be competitive**: differentiate yourself from others and have the customer buy from your company and not from another, because your

product or service is better than the competition's, or because it seems that way to the customer (either because of the product itself, or because of the combination of the variables of the marketing mix discussed in the previous chapter).

2.  **Be profitable** (and, therefore, make money): specifically, it is more focused on reducing the costs of the product or service (without affecting salaries), that is, generating greater productivity. In fact, we can say that 80% of the personnel costs of a company are occupied by operations personnel.

3.  **Be efficient**: if with your management and control of operations you are able to use fewer resources to achieve the same end, the product or service being effective at all times, it will result in the previous objective and you will be more productive and, therefore, more profitable.

Despite what many may think a priori, operations management is a complex business science, as it is based on multidisciplinary management. It is made up of a set of knowledge areas that are completely different from each other and which must be known precisely in this way, as a whole and in detail, in order to ensure the correct decision making of the company's managers and executives and to optimize productivity and achieve the highest levels of competitiveness in the designed strategy.

The activities that contemplate operations management always exist in any company, whether it is a factory, a hotel or driving a taxi (Ries, 2011). It does not matter if it is an industrial or a service company: they all have the function of operations.

One thing that often happens to entrepreneurs is that they tend to neglect the analysis of the stages and operations that take place in the entire cycle of production or service provision (Hagel *et al.*, 2015). To avoid this, you must have a good operations plan and consider that it has to meet the following requirements:

*   Consider the constraints of the general environment (raw material supply, labour supply, etc.)
*   Maintain consistency with the marketing plan as a background and the financial plan as a final constraint
*   Identify the logistic processes from the initial design to the distribution of the product or service
*   Analyze the basic and support activities integrated in each process
*   Evaluate in time and cost the material and human resources that intervene in each process, considering subcontracting
*   Analyze the location of the facilities and the capacities of the production teams

Operations cover all activities from the conception of an idea to a satisfied customer acquiring the product or service that responds to that idea. Satisfaction, which is achieved by obtaining the expectations that the customer has of the company (of the product or service), in the short, medium and long term, becomes an operational objective: that the customer buys again.

When the business starts and, therefore, grows, the balance between the preconceived strategy and the operation to be executed daily can get out of control, as the workload and responsibilities increase. This is why it is essential that the entrepreneur forms high-performance teams and starts delegating tasks, even the most important ones. However, this does not mean that they will not be aware of the operation or the obtained results: on the contrary, the challenge in this new stage is to give precise instructions and be able to monitor the key functions that will determine the future of the company.

So, what are those tasks that allow the company to remain in continuous movement towards achieving profitability? Basically, as Beier (2016) shows, they are these five:

1. **Production**: what do you sell? Customer satisfaction is the basis of every successful business, so the first thing to do is to check that you are meeting their demands and expectations. And it all starts with the manufacturing of the products, or the generation of your services. Depending on the direction your start-up is taking, you should review issues such as fixed and variable costs, inventory management, quality standards or delivery times to customers and/or dealers.
2. **Marketing**: as discussed in the previous chapter, here we do not refer only to the promotion of products or services of your start-up, but to decisions on competitive advantages to highlight the selling price, promotional campaigns and the definition of the points of sale (Jiménez-Marín, 2007). Products, no matter how good they are, do not sell themselves: if the business does not have an adequate strategy to link the company's offer with the market, no marketing effort will be successful.
3. **Sales**: here you activate the machinery that will make a potential client decide to buy your products or services. And there is a very important question you should ask yourself: what is the most important factor in the marketing strategy of your business? Once you have identified that key revenue element, you need to make sure that you have everything you need to keep on giving the same results, or even improve them.
4. **Collections**: a sale will not be closed until the money is in your start-up account. However, many entrepreneurs make the mistake of

focusing only on the number of purchase orders or invoices, while the administration area suffers from a lack of liquidity to cover the payroll or basic services. Don't fall into this fatal error, which in the medium term can end your start-up's financial health. To avoid this, review the collection cycle, compare it with the payment cycle of the company's commitments (for example, a credit) and make the necessary adjustments.

5. **Administration**: finally, there is the area that ensures that everyone in the company has the necessary resources to do their job. Every day you must check that the employees comply with their working hours, that the invoices requested by the vendors are generated, that the payments to suppliers are made or that the taxes are paid on time.

Therefore, from here we try to explain the need to develop an operations plan that anticipates the processes that you will develop in your daily activity and that foresees possible issues that will occur in the future of your start-up in the short, medium and long term (Robehmed & Colao, 2013). But why an operations plan? Because it explains in detail the production process that is followed until the final product or, in the same way, the way in which the service is provided. It is a very useful tool for a company, even more so if yours is developed in a rural environment or if it is directly addressed to the rural public, because it allows the following:

1. Specify the aspects related to the production process and detail the required core operations; aspects such as:

    * Set up a clear and understandable organization chart in which each person knows who to contact to solve or report any issue.
    * Delimit the responsibilities of each member of the company. Which tasks are the responsibility of each one? Explain them.
    * Establish coordination mechanisms between the different departments that make up the company, in order to allow cooperation between members and a rapid flow of information.

2. Determine the procurement policy: the relationship with suppliers is one of the most conflictive points. Every company aims to minimize these costs in order to achieve the widest possible margin. Therefore, it is essential to establish:

    * The expected costs (fixed or variable) associated with the activity to be carried out by the company. It is important to differentiate

between the necessary raw materials, semi-finished products or finished products required in the production process or for direct marketing.

- The suppliers with whom to deal, because it is necessary to obtain the most advantageous conditions possible in terms of prices, delivery times and the optimum quantity of required raw material.
- Where to store the stocks, in case of product manufacturing, or need of raw material that can be stored for your service, as every warehouse has a maximum capacity that cannot be exceeded. In addition, it involves a cost that you must minimize. On the other hand, it is essential to have a minimum remainder to avoid a break in stock in the event of a lack of supply.
- What method of stock valuation should you use? There are three basic methods for valuing stocks:

  a.  FIFO (First In, First Out): the stock leaving the warehouse is valued according to the cost of the oldest one.
  b.  LIFO (Last In, First Out): the stock leaving the warehouse is valued according to the cost of the last one to enter.
  c.  Weighted Average Price: the stock leaving the warehouse is valued according to the average cost of the stock in the warehouse.

- Manage quality, because, as an entrepreneur and future business-person, you must ensure that your product or service meets minimum standards or requirements of expectations. This is especially true if you are operating in a rural environment, as customers know each other.
- Indicate the required technology: you should consider, a priori, what type of technology you will use and its most important characteristics, as well as the state of the technology market and its future prospects, because a technological improvement often means, in the long term, a saving in costs; other times, the fact that the technology disappears can be a disaster for your product or service.
- Take into account the necessary and available human resources. You will have to consider aspects such as:

  a.  Required number of workers.
  b.  Job description: that there is a clear delimitation of the tasks for each member of your start-up.
  c.  Required training and experience, especially if you prefer to train someone young or, on the contrary, you prefer already trained people and with more experience.

d. Communication skills: in case you must transfer knowledge or organize teams, it is essential that you know how to communicate and make the explanation to the group.

• Specify the environmental issues included in the legislation, as well as those that you voluntarily want to follow in your start-up. Above all and considering that your field is rural, you must indicate:

a. Preventive environmental measures and their corresponding cost.
b. The activity carried out by the company with reference to the regulations on environmental protection.
c. Possible corrective measures in case of violation of regulations and/or possible complaint.

## References

Beier, M. (2016). *Startups' Experimental Development of Digital Marketing Activities. A Case of Online-Videos*. 14th Interdisciplinary European Conference on Entrepreneurship Research (IECER), Chur, Switzerland.

Blank, S. (2013). Why the Lean Start-Up Changes Everything? *Harvard Business Review*, 91(5), pp. 63–72.

Blank, S.; Dorf, B. (2012). *The Startup Owner's Manual*. Palo Alto: K&S Ranch Consulting Editorial.

Hagel, J.; Brown, J.; Kulasooriya, D.; Giffi, C.; Chen, M. (2015). *The Future of Manufacturing—Making Things in a Changing World*. London: Deloitte University Press.

Jiménez-Marín, G. (2007). Creación de empresas informativas. En Caro González, F.J. (Ed.), *Gestión de empresas informativas*. Madrid: McGraw Hill.

Ries, E. (2011). *The Lean Startup: How Today's Entrepreneurs Use Continuous Innovation to Create Radically Successful Businesses*. London: Random House LLC.

Robehmed, N.; Colao, J.J. (2013). *What Is a Startup?* Retrieved from www.forbes.com/sites/natalierobehmed/2013/12/16/what-is-a-startup/ [Accessed on 01/06/2020].

# 5 Assembling a Tech Team

*Emilio Solís Bueno and*
*Álvaro Pareja Domínguez*

## Introduction

Nowadays, technology is a key factor in almost every company, especially in a start-up, and so is its management. However, the right profiles for this role are usually the most difficult profiles to find and that can complicate everything. Launching a new product or service will be challenging for you even if you've got an IT geek on board. But wait, it will be even worse if you've got more than one!

If you're waiting for the big, undisclosed secrets of tech start-up success, relax and let's see why most of the things they've told you about start-ups, technology and success are rubbish and post-truth.

## First It Happens, Then You Give It an Explanation

Have you ever gotten five tails in a row by flipping a coin? Luck or probability? Well, that poker face, mixing joy, surprise and self-confidence, is the same one that we have seen in many of the entrepreneurs who have achieved 'success'.

But . . . what if you don't get it again? Maybe get the coin again and throw it hard with rage? What about trying the flip again and again? That is when you start looking for an explanation of why it happened once.

Our brain tries to find patterns all the time, whatever the outcome, but the only truth is that we first watch reality happening in all its greatness and then just try to explain it with our simple patterns.

As entrepreneurship is scary, we try to minimize the incoming 'screw ups' by accumulating recommendation, advice, 'magic' formulas. . . . Again, we try to find patterns (Cooney, 2005).

Don't try to find an explanation. We don't do it either. Each one does their best to write errorless code, to launch viral campaigns . . . but 99% of those explanations, theories and aftermath are nothing more than poorly rationalized reality. Bullshit.

Only 1% get to really uncover a cause-effect based on experience and data and won't easily reveal their 'know how'. Thus, you'd better not believe anything beyond this point. They are just our best patterns.

## Endemic Tech Wildlife

If you can give a face to your CTO (Chief Tech Officer) you are lucky: almost every start-up considers this role as a must in their teams, especially if your project is built over an online platform, mobile app, and so on. However, danger is all around, so you could find it useful to identify certain breeds in the IT wildlife.

### *The 'Don't Get Me Out of My Box' Breed*

If you've heard expressions like 'I'm not going to go that way or the whole thing will become a total mess', then chances are you have a 'solo player' on your team.

As self-centred, they jeopardize decision making when it affects technology. Although caring about the development team, they don't accept externally imposed newcomers (they are a threat to 'their code').

Any new functionality that doesn't match their own priorities is questioned.

They are jealous of a well appreciated 'technical intimacy', either because of mistrust (others could copy) or because of their own limitations (others could carry out). Although surrounded by a technical elite, this person can directly influence potential competitors who would be thrown out of the nest at the first opportunity.

### *The 'You Are With Me or Against Me' Breed*

This time you could be hearing 'we'll do the product launch when I'm ready' or 'if we don't do it this way . . . leave me out of this'.

Sometimes these kind of people become stars.

People like this live on causing a strong fear in others (dropping that they could be eventually leaving the company), or just on the lack of guts around them.

Self-recognized as essential to the company and having courage enough to defy most of the rest, they exercise a blatant coercion that turns the CTO into a 'de facto' CEO. The company becomes 'technocentric' and the rest of the areas 'swear allegiance' to this mindset, which usually causes a brutal disconnection from customer needs.

### The 'Proud to Be a Nerd' Breed

If you've heard sentences like 'The last to merge their part today is hosting the next Warhammer session at home!' or 'You missed one of the agile antipatterns during the last sprint and that's unacceptable!', it's probably too late for you.

You can see cooperative decision making within the group, but also unhealthy product bias. These guys share more than just coding, but hobbies and a whole lifestyle, pretending other non-aligned profiles don't even exist.

The problem about this is a severe lack of diversity in the company.

More than a start-up, the group looks like part of an episode of *The Big Bang Theory* or Silicon Valley.

Just like the TV show, if somebody still stands 'sane' (usually a female member of the group), she is absolutely ignored and hardly manages to influence the culture of the company. It doesn't matter . . . they live happy and free in their own personal nerdland!

## Five Stages of Tech Grief

Whether you didn't ever get a CTO on board or if you just lost them, you'll face the five stages of grief: denial, anger, bargaining, depression and acceptance. So, following some authors (Kamm & Nurick, 1993; Stewart, 1989; Witt, 2004), we can offer a few highlights.

### Denial

In the beginning, you aren't even fully conscious about the problem you are facing. By default, we are all more than capable of achieving success. No one is really essential.

> 'It's a pity that our CTO left the company, but he wasn't so important for the project'.
> 'They spent the whole day on their own and weren't adding up much, apart from technology'.
> 'We can achieve the same in less time and money just using WordPress and a couple of plugins'.

This first stage of denial will perhaps help you alleviate the impact of this kind of loss, or maybe defer it, but all this behaviour is simply exposing that 'fools rush in where angels fear to tread'. Probably your first reaction to this will be to try it yourself: the DIY approach.

Doing it yourself is okay as a temporary solution, or when at the earliest stages of validation and development. All respect for those pros devoting thousands of 'flight hours' to make all sorts of complex solutions look easy!

However, it is NOT a bad idea that you make incursions into that space from time to time, just for 'breaking the ice': make your own WordPress site (adapt a theme, build a landing page, embed tracking code in it, etc.). These are easy tasks that could be useful during the first 'baby steps' along with your start-up, when validation and speed are what could be really moving the needle.

For sure, it'll help you to better assess and appreciate a good tech job.

## *Anger*

Everything is plug and play until you do it yourself; you'll become a victim of frustration.

> 'I spent a whole week just to have this landing page ready! This won't be sustainable'.

Feelings of anger, resentment and frustration at irreversible loss is projected onto close people on a professional and personal level, so it's easy for you to even take the problem 'home'. It's happened to all of us. Watch out for the consequences.

It will be in these moments when the strength of the team is tested, because the 'bad mood' will put pressure on the start-up members and will bring out any latent fissures. You won't be surprised to know that the main cause of death for incipient businesses is not around the lack of financing or market difficulties, but rather issues with founders.

What doesn't kill you makes you stronger, right? We'd add that this is a required process in every start-up.

## *Bargaining*

Once blood pressure drops, your rational side will try to save the situation with ingenuity and creativity. At this point there is some controversy: some call this 'resilience' and consider it one of the fundamental virtues of the entrepreneur. Others simply think that it is just being a 'bad loser' and that also ends up meaning a waste of time. You have to give yourself time to fix things, but no more.

This time you will enter the 'forest of possibilities':

> 'What if we outsource development to another company?'

'Or we can hire a couple of interns to begin with, right?'
'What if we post an offer on one of those freelancing sites? They are used to doing this kind of stuff for third parties'.

In this phase you will fantasize with the idea that the situation can be reversed or changed. Be careful; despair can lead you to do terrible things like hiring technology consultants (unsupervised), leaving development to the fellows (unsupervised) or using 'freelancing' (unsupervised) websites.

Even if you're desperate, don't do it. The risk is too high. You should only use these alternatives in a staggered and supervised manner. Some lucky people have reported success about early outsourcing, but many more reported a total waste of time and resources. Failure is not as noisy.

You should only hire a technology consultant to develop your web platform, mobile app, and so on if you already have a CTO, or your technology will be kidnapped by third parties.

The same approach applies in the matter of 'freelancers' (basically it is also a way to outsource): if there is no one with a technical profile within your team, it is very difficult to communicate, not only technically, but add language and distance to that. If you pay with peanuts, you'll end up hiring monkeys.

The same is also true if you have interns without a CTO guiding them, using the same 'language': it is a bad scenario. They aren't usually ready yet to deal with the full responsibility of development.

### *Depression*

The time to 'feel down' came. Here you are, about to ride the roller coaster of entrepreneurship at full speed, free fall direct to hell. There's no hope.

'This is a disaster! It is going to cost us a lot of money and it doesn't even look like what we had in mind. Maybe we won't even launch'.
'In the end I am acting also as CTO, dealing with interns, frustrated and leaving behind what I could do better considering my experience'.

You may feel sad or empty because these are emotions linked to the natural desolation before an important setback. You must take care of the consequences of that state of mind: isolation and lack of motivation. You must hold on as it is!

It's not worth stopping at this point anymore. There's not much else to do and you won't feel like doing much more, either.

*Acceptance*

Even the longest night comes to an end! In the end we must accept what happened and go through it. Watch out! This process is not automatic and you must learn to 'really' accept what happened and gain new forces to move on. Otherwise, you could get depressed 'in a loop' and that would not be good. Dude, this is true resilience!

> 'Okay! We need a CTO. Where's the next "geeky" event?'
> 'We need someone who understands technology and is involved in the company, even if they are not fully dedicated at first. Someone must look out for our interests'.
> 'We will adapt to this situation as long as we find the right person'.

Once the new reality is accepted, we learn to live with it and gradually bring hope and positivism back, and the desire to move on. It is important to get some positive learning from the mistakes. We mean things like improving planning, striving to learn how to 'ask' (collect the right requirements for the product to be developed) and so on.

Of course, you should keep trying to hire a CTO profile, although not at any price or in any way. The key is to understand that it works like any other relationship: you must build trust and take steps as this relationship consolidates. If you are good in love, you will understand what we mean. If you are not, find someone on your team who is and delegate!

In this case, you should not make the mistake of offering stock or a very high salary when the relationship is not strong enough, or you'll never know if it's true love.

Of course, the task is not easy; you must carefully manage the expectations of the other party. First, so that you don't feel tied by promises you made to earn their trust but must keep later. Second, an overdemanding scenario in the technological labour market tends to lead to greater turnover (people just 'jumping' to improve benefits with each new contract), so it will be equally important to achieve a higher engagement from them while using some creativity, increasing the emotional salary they get.

If everything goes well, once you have the right profile, you will have to work every single day to fine tune that wonderful living mechanism called your start-up. Let's talk about ways to work a little better.

## The New 'New' Tech Product Development

For those people who slightly know the focus of agile development, this title might sound familiar, because it honours the one published by Takeuchi and Nonaka in 1986 in *Harvard Business Review*, named 'The New New Product Development Game', where they settled down the bases of the incoming agile development framework known as Scrum.

Sadly, some things are still new 'new' even decades later. While unbelievable, the number of start-ups (and businesses) that still use obsolete methodologies nowadays, with a linear development concept and pyramid-like organization in order to carry out their technological development, is scary: traditional 'waterfall' project management, teams being 'tyrannized' by a project leader who doesn't even want to be there, performance metrics based on attendance or how many code lines were generated, and so on.

It's been a long time since I realized that a start-up must be different from a traditional software development company in several ways—from scratch! If we as a start-up share all the cons of a traditional business (lack of flexibility, obsolete methodology, etc.) but can't count on any of their pros (more workers, more resources, more contacts, more contracts, etc.), then failure is guaranteed. Because of this, a start-up should adopt an agile development approach as part of its competitive strategy. With this in place, it could now compete in a better way even with less resources available, because it became a flexible, efficient and high-performing team (Boone *et al.*, 2019).

We'll go further: this agile focus does not apply only to the development team, but to the whole company. Of course, product development will benefit from embracing this lifestyle and you're warned . . . it won't be easy, but this would almost immediately lower the inherent friction coming out of the usually rough relationship between business and tech areas. Every start-up is actually just an agile development team trying to move the uncertainty out of its way to bring a solution into the market in the most successful manner.

Other methodologies like Lean Start-Up or Design Thinking share both an interactive (co-creation along with potential customers) and iterative approach (empiricism, trial and error), so this mindset easily adapts to the challenges of a starting business project: trying out several customer segments until finding the needs really worth solving, constant changes in the user profile to reflect trends, habits and so on, designs and redesigns rapidly made into prototypes offering limited functionality to have early feedback from our first 'victims', and so on.

The principles of agile development keep the essence of the main skills and techniques to use for achieving a great technological development in a start-up environment.

### No 'Silos', Please

Whether you are the CEO, CMO, CTO or just the last intern to arrive, all of you are part of a team. Even if you have very specific expertise, it is crucial that you contribute with your own knowledge, experience and commitment, even to tasks that aren't necessarily related to your profile, when we're talking about priority challenges for the company. Learning to collaborate in every context is key in order to optimize the few resources that the start-up has from the very beginning. If we talk about technology, even if you don't know a thing about programming or design and usability, I'm sure you could always help with adding some effort to the whole team from your own point of view. That's what makes a group become a real team.

### *Rename the Key Areas of Your Start-Up*

Why set up roles the traditional way? No management, technology, marketing or finances! Be flexible. Use the challenges that are key in every moment for going to the next level. If your priority now is developing a functional prototype for the first demos, attract your first customers to that demo and look for some financing to make the 'death valley' crossing a bit easier, then your departments would be three: prototype development, early adopters onboarding and seed funding. Each area must have a leader, but again, be careful with silos! The leader in each area must have an overall vision and be able to coordinate the efforts to progress in those areas, but that doesn't mean the leader must do all the work. For example, a technological profile could help develop the prototype for a mobile app but could also be helpful in getting new customers just by attending meetings to share specific technical info or sharing it into the documentation to be delivered to investors or to raise public funding.

### *No Bosses, Please*

Founders own the power to completely change the course of the company, but at a functional level companies turn out to be better when running as self-organized teams where knowledge, experience and natural leadership matter more than processes or discipline. This isn't something reserved only for developers. To work well, a development team must aggregate the commitment from all its members and for this to happen, a certain level of shared understanding must be reached about what the role everyone is playing or should have is and what battles to fight. They clearly apply most principles of a sports team's internal organization. Just like a scrum team.

### *Clear and Shared Focus and Method*

Of course, you'll need a clear focus in order to get the product released. You'll soon realize that those products offering thousands of weird, niche-catching functionalities tailored to the taste of the dev team leader look directly into the abyss of failure, as they totally ignore the customer and their needs. It's also clear that you'll need some method to be able to get your team to work properly, it being more or less chaotic, depending on the case. Every teammate has a different focus point and their own ways of working. The real problem is communication.

The best investment (in time) you can make in a start-up is about defining a clear and shared focus point, flowing out of a well-defined and shared work method and collaboration. It doesn't matter if you simply don't follow the canons of a certain methodology, as it usually evolves quite naturally into a shared and agreed upon version. The rest is a matter of time and the only restriction is that you also figure out how to improve this way of working continuously.

# References

Boone, C.; Lokshin, B.; Guenter, H.; Belderbos, R. (2019). Top Management Team Nationality Diversity, Corporate Entrepreneurship and Innovation in Multinational Firms. *Strategic Management Journal*, 40, pp. 277–302.

Cooney, T.M. (2005). What Is an Entrepreneurial Team? *International Small Business Journal*, pp. 226–235.

Kamm, J.B.; Nurick, A.J. (1993). The Stages of Team Venture Formation: A Decision-Making Model. *Entrepreneurship Theory and Practice*, 17(2), pp. 17–27.

Stewart, A. (1989). *Team Entrepreneurship*. Milwaukee: Marquette University.

Witt, P. (2004). Entrepreneurs' Networks and the Success of Start-Ups. *Entrepreneurship and Regional Development*, 16(5), pp. 391–413.

# 6  Legal Tips for Newcomers

*Víctor López Pérez and Ricardo San Martín*

## Introduction

Nine out of ten start-ups fail in their first 3 years of life. If you are one of the newcomers to this exciting but difficult world of entrepreneurship, we advise you to focus on minimizing those risks that you will undoubtedly find from the first moments of your project's life. There is nothing worse than a good idea that is dead before it is born for reasons that could have been avoided.

Among those risks are, as you can imagine from the title of the chapter, those of a legal nature, due to one of the most common mistakes when starting a commercial type of project, which is to think that we will not need lawyers until we start billing.

By the time we finally start exchanging money for our innovative products or services, we will have already had to decide on many issues that seem key to the survival of our business in the short, medium and long term.

The first and most important is related to the role and obligations of each of the partners in the development of business activity. Commonly answering the most basic questions on this point is essential to avoid friction within the team. Yes, we are talking about reflecting in a document, and in detail, the agreements that the partners have reached among themselves, as Fox and Wade-Benzoni explained (2017).

But not only that. Today, many businesses operate with complex, innovative tax structures that need review and the input of legal advisors to help your team build the product without structural failure. You cannot validate a business model without knowing if it meets with current legislation in the territory where you plan to run it. There are very good ideas that are enforceable in Malta but not in Spain, for example, because the legislation is not the same in these countries.

On the other hand, the execution of ideas and bringing them to life come from brilliant, restless minds who have seen their lightbulb light up at a certain point in the night and have run to write them down in a notebook, instead of going to see an expert advisor in intellectual and industrial property. This is followed by financing rounds, innumerable meetings and networking events where, innocently looking for resources and relationships to be able to start their project, these idea-makers provide more information than recommended and, what is worse, without being protected. What is the consequence? An identical product or service is born, driven by a perhaps less brilliant but more clever mind. The advice of this point is clear: protect your idea.

If you have established a good partnership agreement, you have legally and fiscally validated your potential business and you are covered by the registration of your innovative idea, you will be in a safe position to sit down with potential investors who want to get on the boat. It will be a long and wave-laden journey, so the advice is not to let anyone go on deck and examine it thoroughly before making any decision. You have to do this preliminary examination, analyzing your needs from a financial point of view, but also taking into consideration other positive points that you would like to see your partners be a part of (Wade-Benzoni *et al.*, 2010).

Right now, and more than ever: don't go without your legal advisor, and don't sign any document, not even a simple nondisclosure agreement (NDA).

As you can see, having a legal advisor from the very beginning of your business idea seems vital to eliminate at one fell swoop many of those risks that are inherent to commercial traffic. It is life insurance against problems that can ruin the good start of an innovative project. Now we will try to give you some identifying tips so that you can choose a lawyer who becomes part of the solution and never part of the problem.

## Some Pieces of Advice

Stay away from big law firms and gentlemen with uniformed Dior ties. You will be paying for a structure that is obsolete and has been living on borrowed time, which you do not need. Focus on finding a professional integrated into a volatile, dynamic structure who can serve you at any time and from any point on the face of the Earth. Find a lawyer who was born in the digital age, who understands the importance of the personal data you will handle and who practices preventive counselling; especially the prosecutor. This type of professional isn't cheap, but at least you'll be paying for quality advice not executed by a junior profile.

Find a lawyer who offers you complete and compact services. A team that deals with the legal, tax, accounting and labour aspects of your business is the best thing to do to clear your head of trouble, so you can focus on the one thing you need for your start-up to survive and succeed: scale and bill.

Look for that lawyer who does not ask you for permanence but who charges you in the first consultation you make. Stay away from those who offer you services for free, as they are reflecting the little value that their services have in the market. Ask the lawyer to show you the portfolio of companies he advises and, if you can, ask for references before hiring him or her. Don't be afraid to try to identify the most suitable lawyer for your project and when you find them, make them an inseparable part of your team. Give them the keys to each room of your project so that they know it in depth.

Stay away from braggarts and from company mentors who have never run one, and be with those who rarely attend people-sponsored events. All they say is 'you can' in children's team games by sticking Post-its on white walls. All the (successful) start-ups that we have advised together with our team in the last 10 years are made up of people addicted to the search for perfection and who, as far as possible, avoid spending time on procedures and events that do not help your business become more effective and profitable, such as idea competitions and similar events with zero added value.

The world of entrepreneurship is a bubble about to burst and those who have built foundations capable of adapting to the storms and winds at any moment will be behind it. We can understand storms and winds, for example, a pandemic like the one we have experienced in the year 2020. We must be anti-fragile and come out reinforced from the complex situations that we must live in, embracing each difficulty to make ourselves stronger and, if possible, wiser. Understanding and pursuing anti-fragility, Taleb's supine concept, will inevitably lead you to seek the best possible human capital for your business journey and this will undoubtedly include a young, prepared, honest and transparent legal team (Hervas-Oliver & Roberto, 2017).

## Frequent Errors You Should Not Fall Into

Here are some of the common mistakes among early entrepreneurs and we will give you our opinion on them. Assess the situation and avoid these pitfalls as much as possible:

1. **Setting up the company after the activity has started**. Mistake. Do not wait to legally incorporate the entity once you have started to operate, but from the first moment, because from the first moment you are incurring expenses that you could include in your accounting and deduct from the tax point of view. Every time you meet with a third party (supplier, potential client or investors) you are operating and sometimes incurring obligations. It becomes easier and cheaper to create and incorporate such activity as a company form and, in the medium and long term, you will benefit.

2.  **Do not fail to make a partnership agreement**. Mistake. Make a partnership agreement early on, even if your partners are your best friends and you trust them completely. We have seen partners who seemed to be more than just friends become the worst enemies by losing not only the project, but huge amounts of resources, such as time and money, along the way. A legal agreement between partners should be your priority and it should set all those aspects that regulate that agreement, which you have reached between you to make your project grow.

3.  **Not obtaining legal advice**. Mistake. Get advice as soon as you can, because not having it is the most frequent mistake and it may be that without the intervention of a legal advisor your goods, your idea or your service may never see the light of day or, what is worse, it may start to work in an inappropriate way and, once it is launched, you may find yourself running into a wall of problems impossible to jump over.

4.  **Not registering an idea, patent or utility model**. Mistake. Ideas and products can be copied relatively easily, especially in today's knowledge society where communications are very fluid between different parts of the planet. This is a very common mistake that derives from an excessive confidence in those involved in the global market and that translates into the appropriation of ideas in the early stages of the project. This error of not protecting creations is observed in new entrepreneurs and rarely in investors or entrepreneurs of second projects with experience.

# References

Fox, M.; Wade-Benzoni, K. (2017). The Creation of Opportunity Is an Opportunity to Create: Entrepreneurship as an Outlet for the Legacy Motive. *Research in Organizational Behaviour*, 37, pp. 167–184.

Hervas-Oliver, J.L.; Roberto Cervello, M.L. (2017). The Dynamics of Cluster Entrepreneurship: Knowledge Legacy from Parents or Agglomeration Effects? The Case of the Castellon Ceramic Tile District. *Research Policy*, 46(1), pp. 73–92.

Wade-Benzoni, K.A.; Sondak, H.; Galinsky, A.D. (2010), Leaving a Legacy: Intergenerational Allocations of Benefits and Burdens. *Business Ethics Quarterly*, 20(2010), pp. 7–34.

# 7    Dealing (and Working) With Large Companies

*Óscar Carreras and Patricia Hernanz Falcón*

## Introduction

When we begin to work autonomously and independently, that is, for ourselves, by undertaking, we can find certain limitations that, on a great number of occasions, start from ideas that lack a real basis. This makes us distrust our project and, when it comes to growing, we can fall into underestimating our company.

When we grow, we do so thanks to external entities: suppliers, customers, investors, potential partners and so on. Here are some guidelines to ensure that your promotion and collaboration with other entities is successful.

## Phases

Whether you are an entrepreneur looking for new clients or a person interested in working for a company, the process consists of three fundamental phases (López Rodríguez *et al.*, 2020; Yea *et al.*, 2018; Williams, 2015; Barabino *et al.*, 2012):

1.  **Research phase**: choose the entity you are going to address. Here it is essential to consider the following issues:

    *   **Company size**: working with large companies has many advantages, but it is more important to evaluate what type of entity will benefit most from your proposal, because a product can work very well in one company, but not in another. A small company today may be a multinational tomorrow, so this factor should not affect your final decision.
    *   **Company culture**: working with a company means a lot of hours spent every day interacting with the people who make it up, so if you want the professional relationship to last over time, it is essential to connect with the way they work.

- **Commercial benefit of your proposal for that company**: whether your proposal is a new technology or product or consists of improving a process within the company, you should focus on the commercial benefit you would be bringing to that company: a direct economic benefit, for example, by increasing the number of sales thanks to your innovative product or technology; or an indirect economic benefit, for example, by improving processes that will make the company more efficient, which will translate into a reduction in costs and, therefore, an improvement in profits in the medium or long term.

2. **Contact phase**: you must decide how to contact the company and the format of presentation. Once the research phase has been completed and you have decided which company is your target, you have to prepare the strategy for contacting the company. In this sense, we would like to clarify that there is no magic formula that will work, as there are many factors that will contribute to the interest of the person you are going to contact in your proposal, but you should certainly consider:

   - **Contact the right person**: the criteria should be the department they work in and their ability to make decisions within that department. If you contact someone without decision-making power, you will waste your time. If you contact someone in the wrong department, it won't work either. Thanks to social networks and LinkedIn, you can easily find the right person for your purpose.
   - **Be concise**: nobody has time to read a 20-page dossier. Give a brief introduction to your product, explain what benefits it would bring to the company and how, and finish with a couple of sentences explaining why you chose that company.
   - **Don't limit yourself to one form of contact**: try at least three to get started: email, message through LinkedIn and speak in person at an event.
   - **Networking**: it is essential and the best way to get an opportunity, either because your contact knows someone at the company you are interested in and can help you locate someone on the inside, or because they work at that company and you can present them with a quick proposal on the spot. Events are a perfect opportunity to meet people and get your idea across to the right people.
   - **Don't lose hope and keep trying**: think that you will be rejected in most cases and that this is the natural process for everyone who tries, but there will always be someone interested. So be patient and don't throw in the towel.

3.  **Implementation phase**: this phase is not necessarily the most impor-
    tant phase, but it is the time when you will convince the company that
    they need you. And that's when you present your project.

    Once the chosen company has decided to listen to your proposal, you
    have only one chance to convince them that they need you, so don't
    miss it:

    - In the research phase you should have learned everything about that
      company: what they do and why, what their values are, if there are
      commercial gaps that could be covered with your proposal, what
      products they offer, what their business model is.
    - It is also essential to do a market study, to understand the financial
      needs and the current social, political and technological compo-
      nents and to integrate them into your strategy.
    - For your presentation to be satisfactory, we recommend that it
      should offer a clear structure and be concise, but with a level of
      detail appropriate for that first presentation.
    - Anticipate any problems that may arise during the day:

        - Carry the presentation in various formats: PowerPoint and
          PDF on the computer, on a pen drive, in the cloud and on
          paper. And, if necessary, on Egyptian papyrus.
        - Plan your trip to the area where the company is located to arrive
          at least half an hour in advance. Traffic or transport failures are
          common and there is nothing worse than being late for a meeting.
        - If the presentation is via video conference, which is very com-
          mon in a first contact with the company, keep your computer
          and mobile phone at hand and have a plan B in case the Inter-
          net fails at that time.

    - Prepare yourself mentally for that day: you need to be clear about
      what the objective of that day is and focus on getting that message
      across. The more prepared you are, the less nerves will arise that
      day, so do your homework. And, of course, trust yourself. At the
      end of the day, you are the person who knows the most about your
      product/initiative.
    - Take this opportunity to ask yourself about the company, as they
      will be evaluating you, but you should still decide if that company
      is the right choice for your business.
    - Don't forget to send a follow-up email after the presentation thank-
      ing them for their time and showing your interest in continuing the
      negotiations.

- Good luck! Every professional success requires a lot of effort, but also a small dose of luck.

Finally, we would like to highlight a fundamental factor: enjoy the opportunity; there is nothing that works better than showing your passion and knowledge, and that is best achieved when you are having fun. Remember that companies bet on new ideas, but above all on the person behind the new proposal. So be yourself and show them what you are worth!

## Other Reflections

### *People Behind People*

Behind these corporations there are only people who want to share their experiences with you and learn from you. And you realize that what binds you to them is much more than what separates you.

So, if you want to talk to a business giant because you have an idea or a project that you think will interest them, don't think of the 'giant' as such; think of the people you are going to talk to:

- Develop your network because through your network you will have more possibilities that the person will listen to you because there will be someone who will serve as a bridge.
- Try to find the things that bring you together by looking at Google, LinkedIn, Facebook and so on. When you know what unites you, you will feel more relaxed and you will always be able to break the ice by talking about these things. Also, remember that during the presentation, your nonverbal communication represents 90% of your communication.
- Believe in your project and your value proposal. No one knows your project better than you do and it must be part of your DNA. When you believe in something you try it until the end, you learn from your mistakes and you get up as many times as you need to.
- And don't forget to listen actively and ask questions when you have doubts. If you want to work with them or work for them, remember that asking is a sign of interest.
- Persevere. Entrepreneurs must be able to deal with obstacles. A business is not built overnight; it takes time. You must get used to people saying no to you.
- Don't compare yourself to anyone else in this world. If you do, you are insulting yourself: when you spend your time and energy trying to analyze other people's perceptions of you, you get stuck.

### The Leader Is the One Who Makes You Feel That You Are Important

The necessary attributes to be a good leader are learned with experience, a lot of dedication, great effort and a lot of humility. Learning from your environment, from those around you and from your own and others' successes and failures will make you understand others better and be a better worker, a better entrepreneur and a better boss, if applicable.

Keep all this in mind when addressing a giant because, although this produces respect (and sometimes fear), remember that the great giants began as seeds.

### People Will Forget What You Told Them, But Never What You Made Them Feel

Certain personal attributes such as verbal communication or critical thinking are vital to success in the business world. But also important are nonverbal communication, empathy and the ability to transport people to the place where you want to take them. Because professional and personal relationships are very similar, we all tend to group together with people who have a similar vision to ours. Feeling good with others makes us more open to discuss any issue and the feeling of teamwork flourishes. Corporations are not oblivious to all these factors. And so, the creation of teams within companies is intended to bring together people who have very distinct qualities but who can work together to develop valuable activities.

## References

Barabino, B.; Salis, S.; Assorgia, A. (2012). Application of Mobility Management: A Web Structure for the Optimisation of the Mobility of Working Staff of Big Companies. *Institution of Engineering and Technology*, 6(1), pp. 87–95. https://doi.org/10.1049/iet-its.2010.0168.

López Rodríguez, A.; Jiménez-Marín, G.; Torres García, M.; Giesecke, S.; Morales Conde, I. (2020). *Historias de Emprendimiento Andaluz en Silicon Valley*. Sevilla: McGraw Hill.

Williams, S. (2015). More Than Data: Working with Big Data for Civics. *Journal of Law and Policy for the Information Society*, 181, pp. 1–2.

Yea, Z.; Hassana, A.; TAlibb, H.; Hea, J. (2018). Analyzing the Differentiation Strategies of Big Companies Competing with Each Other. *Strategic Management*, 23(3), pp. 25–37. https://doi.org/10.5937/StraMan1803025Z25-37.

# Part II

# Entrepreneurship With Rural Start-Ups

To give more perspective, and to be able to provide current or future entre-preneurs with a real perspective of rural entrepreneurship in different places, we have proceeded to contact a series of start-ups that have told us about their experiences.

They have done so through three questions that we have considered to be key. We hope that they are interesting and that they can help entrepreneurs.

All start-ups have answered these three questions:

**1st Question:** Where did you start? Did you feel there were disadvan-tages compared to other start-ups who started in the big hubs? (What are, in your opinion, the differences between the entrepreneurial eco-system where you started and the famous ones?)

**2nd Question:** How did you adapt to your environment (first steps, team building and first customers)?

**3rd Question:** What would you change if you could go back in time (advice for entrepreneurs in rural areas)?

# 8   Spain

*Coordinator: Patricia López Trabajo*

*Acknowledgements: Celia Polo*

## 360° Heritage

**Pitch:** 360° Heritage is an engine that builds digital tours with Google Streetview images that track the users' preferences.
**Author/s:** Alejandro López Rodríguez (CEO), Raúl Díez Martínez and Umberto León Domínguez (mentors).
**Location:** Spain, Seville, Olivares.

### *1st Question*

In my opinion, although success depends basically on personal commitment, talent and endeavour (and luck!), the environment plays a major role in developing opportunities.

The good news is that even if you don't have a strong ecosystem around you, it will not stop you from achieving great things. It will just take more time and effort.

In my case, starting a technological venture from a little village in the very south of Spain may not sound like the greatest idea, especially if you are neither a technical person yourself, nor have the money to hire one. To make things more complicated, I also had to stay enclosed in my village to support my family and look after my father, who had a degenerative disease.

My entrepreneurial experience started during the years where start-ups and tech entrepreneurship were beginning to take off with all the fireworks and propaganda from Silicon Valley. All these Steve Jobs biographies, Facebook movies and so on. In a matter of months, many initiatives from the government arose to motivate people to create start-ups and to believe in themselves, just as we read every day in the news from Silicon Valley, amplified by sites like Twitter and LinkedIn. Everyone was talking about how cool it was to have a start-up. In theory, that sounds great, but the truth is that the slogans, the facilities and the propaganda can be imitated, but not the resources. So many of these initiatives were a waste of time, others were experiments and only a few worked.

## 2nd Question

I had the luck to have my project granted by the university, so I could visit Rocket Space in San Francisco (the accelerator where Uber and Spotify were) for one month. The key learnings were:

1.  I had to be my own team. I had to learn to do everything for myself, from business to coding (it took me two years full time to code proficiently). I had to find a very concrete need that my product could fit and put all my (small) strength on that. I had to be like a sniper.
2.  There was no market for my solution in my area, so I had to sell it abroad. My product had to be in English first.
3.  I had to be very picky with the people I listened to when I came back to my country. Not everyone who sell themselves as experts are really experts. But to identify who was fake or not, I needed to first build a foundation myself.

When I returned home, I signed up for some online courses in UCLA, then studied mathematics and statistics in Khan Academy and Data Science in Datacamp. All online. Then, with time, I met the people who were worthy to listen to and spent two years, full time, rebuilding my project.

At the UCLA courses I got ten points over the maximum possible marks, then shared it on my social networks and a person I knew from Expedia since my tour guide years asked me what my project was about. They liked it and after nine months adapting it to their needs, now it is part of their digital portfolio. Four–five years married with my project.

## 3rd Question

If I could go back in time, I would say this to myself:

1.  **Learn finances and accounting**: you are building a start-up to make money, so you must understand how it works.
2.  **Learn marketing**: it is a common mistake to think of marketing as 'digital marketing', when 'digital' is only a channel. True marketing is about understanding the needs of the customers and then serving them in any way they find valuable.
3.  **Don't trust any expert just because they have an institution behind them**: be very selective with whom you listen to. Thanks to sites like LinkedIn, it is very easy to track if a person is worth your attention or not.
4.  **Surround yourself with valuable and good people**, people who tell you the truth even if you don't like what they say.

5.  **Be prepared to look for customers outside your area**: don't be afraid to adapt your product to their needs, if it makes sense.

And the last point, if you have a difficult situation at home: if you feel that you are too stressed or overwhelmed by the situation, then stop, take some rest and don't let your personal stuff interfere with your business decisions. Really, stop and rest. You are not a machine.

## Imperfectus

> **Pitch:** Imperfectus distributes seasonal fruits and vegetables that do not meet the cosmetic requirements of big supermarkets and retailers.
> **Author/s:** Oriol Aldoma (CEO).
> **Location:** Spain, Lleida, Bellpuig.

### *1st Question*

We started up our business in Bellpuig (Lleida), a small town in a rural area in the northeast of Spain. Our town has roughly 5,000 inhabitants and most people work in the primary sector. As you might imagine, Bellpuig is not a big entrepreneurial hub.

However, that does not mean that we face disadvantages compared to other big entrepreneurial hubs.

Most people believe that being in a big hub brings many benefits—for example, collaboration with other start-ups, ability to find talent with entrepreneurial spirit, ability to find more resources . . . and we agree. However, in a rapidly changing world that goes towards working from distance and from home, we believe that such collaboration, talent and resources can easily be achieved remotely.

From the beginning of our project, we have embraced working remotely and working from home. We have worked with:

*   Engineers from India and Barcelona to build our website and processes
*   Lawyers from Murcia (east of Spain) to help with trademark and brand
*   A graphic designer from Chile

On the other side, operating from a rural area brings you many benefits:

*   Hiring is significantly cheaper
*   Office costs are significantly below any cities' cost
*   And finally, in the food sector, being in rural areas improves your brand and 'authenticity'—to give you an example: would it feel more natural/

better to buy vegetables and fruit from an online store based in New York City . . . or from a farmer from a small town in Pennsylvania?

## 2nd Question

We adapted our business from the beginning to the rural environment. We knew it would be difficult to find the right talent for very important parts of our business, such as graphic design, website creation and engineering. So, we tried to find talent outside of our environment for areas where we would be able to work remotely.

We worked a lot with Upwork, a company that connects you with free-lancers. Our first freelancer was Anil, from India—he helped us throughout 3 months in the creation of our website. That helped us achieve our objectives with regards to the functionalities of our website.

We have outsourced other areas to people around the country and world, through Upwork and other ways, which has helped us achieve great results and bridge the 'talent' gap from a rural area.

We've also hired a number of employees in our area for the day-to-day of the company—such employees have been very motivated with our project: in a rural area like ours, our project is very unique as there are not many growing start-ups—thus, it becomes very appealing for employees to work with us.

Being 'unique' in our rural area also helped us achieve the first sales: we managed to get a lot of free press coverage in our area and customers felt more attached to the project and business, as they liked seeing a start-up being created in the area, regardless of the rural stigma.

## 3rd Question

Our advice is that you should not feel disadvantaged by being in a rural area. Hiring talent, collaboration and finding the right resources can easily be found/achieved remotely today.

You should leverage as much as possible all your connections in the rural area: press in the rural area will be very happy to cover a story of an entre-preneur trying to succeed in the area; customers will be thrilled to buy from a growing start-up which is trying to succeed where they live; employees will also be excited to participate in an interesting project in an area where most of the jobs relate to the primary sector.

Be bold, ask questions and travel—seeing the world will allow you to come up with great ideas, learn and implement them in your area when you get back!

# Sunjob

> **Pitch:** We provide quality job opportunities for workers and farmers in the agricultural sector.
> **Author/s:** Manuel Lozano (CEO), Daniel Cabezas (COO), Juan Luis (CMO), Víctor Antón (CTO).
> **Location:** Spain, Badajoz, Villanueva de la Serena.

## *1st Question*

Our idea arose from the need demanded by this sector. On the one hand, Manuel works in a family consultancy and his clients, mostly farmers from 'Las Vegas del Guadiana', came daily demanding agricultural labour. The fruit must be harvested at the precise moment of maturity and farmers did not find such workers when they needed it. On the other hand, Daniel works in a family agricultural holding and, having discussed this issue with Manuel, he could not find workers, so he spent every single day calling people interested in working in this sector.

For this reason, we did not think there could be any downsides. On the contrary, we thought it was an advantage because the need existed here and perhaps, in the big hubs, this demand was ignored or unnoticed.

We live in a business ecosystem closely related to agriculture, which is our main economic engine. The main difference may be the entrepreneurial culture, as most of the companies are very traditional and spend little money on R&D.

## *2nd Question*

Well, when we decided to venture into this project, we started with sketches of the services we wanted to offer. The idea was clear to us; we wanted it to be something simple, fast and effective.

The problem came when we started looking for computer scientists. Some of them did not know how to develop exactly what we wanted and others seemed very expensive to us and we did not have enough money to pay them. To all this we had to add our lack of knowledge about programming and, in general, about application development. It's all Greek to us!

For this reason, we started working together dividing the tasks. We are close friends and we understand each other well. In addition to this, we have also trained in this area, attending start-up acceleration courses and, in a self-taught way, we have tried to solve those problems we were encountering. For example, we already dominate Google Analytics and before we did not even know that it existed.

Our first experience was locally with farmers in our region. We had some meetings with them and they really liked our project. Moreover, we also had meetings with social inclusion associations, obtaining great acceptance from them. Little by little, we began to have users who make use of it and we realized that our project could be successful. However, to face rural customers with a technological project of this level, we must be patient.

### 3rd Question

We think that, if we had to go back in time, we would change how hasty we have been on many occasions, since, by wanting to launch the product as soon as possible, we have been uploading things that did not work perfectly. Consequently, it affected the user experience. We know how difficult it is to get clients in any business and, in our case, the clients are the users. When we had complaints, we tried to solve them as best as possible and, perhaps, that is one of the tasks that has taken us the most time. We have divided the tasks, managing social networks and answering the claims from both the website and WhatsApp. With all this, we have always wanted to demonstrate to users that, although the application might have some bugs, Sunjob is made up of a great human team, which is there to help them in everything that is in our power.

If we had to give some advice to entrepreneurs in rural areas, we would tell them to think as if they were really in that environment. Identifying with issues many people living in rural areas face can lead to offering them a solution, that is, to making business. What is clear is that no one can put themselves in your shoes and no one can offer a solution to something if they haven't suffered it themselves.

We would like to encourage all entrepreneurs and ask them to never lose hope because, although the road is long, work always leads to success.

## MYHIXEL

> **Pitch:** MYHIXEL offers a climax control solution applying the latest technology and gamification to improve men's sexual well-being.
> **Author/s:** Patricia López (CEO).
> **Location:** Spain, Seville, Tomares.

### 1st Question

Definitely developing an idea from scratch and setting up a start-up wasn't easy in Tomares, a medium size village in Seville, due to the lack of start-up culture, experts and other founders around me.

There were very few people in the area who could give us some advice, so we had to constantly take a risk and experiment with most things on our own. We got tips from great experts in business, but we always needed to adapt it into the start-up 'know-how'. As an example, when we started our Kickstarter campaign, there were only two other companies in our region which had launched a campaign in this platform. I am sure we would have had a very different experience in a great hub like Madrid or Barcelona!

The lack of a start-up culture in the region directly affects the investment process. Once we wanted people lother than Family, Fools & Friends (FFF) circle investors to be involved in our project, we had a really hard time finding investors and business angels who understood how a start-up works. Even if our market was the same as if we were based in a big city such as Barcelona, Madrid or London, we were always at lower valuations just because of the region we were based in.

Regarding a start-up founders circle where I could share my experience and learn from others, it was almost impossible. Being in a region where there is no entrepreneurial culture is a great challenge on top of what founding a start-up already is.

### 2nd Question

As a female start-up founder with a project targeted for men, I had many situations where I had to choose to dare and move more than stand still. The south of Spain is a difficult region for entrepreneurs and sometimes I felt we were creating a new spot of economical growth and a new reflection where young people with ideas could look and take as a reference.

Adapting my project to this environment also depended on the team I gathered step by step, where they might not be experts in start-ups, but they had passion and good work to offer. We always keep our minds and eyes open to opportunities, because we never knew where the magic might happen. But at the end, it is crucial to make an effort as a team every day and make it happen more than waiting for it.

### 3rd Question

I wish 'ctrl+z' would exist in real life! It seems easier now that we can look back in time, but back then, I tried to make the most with the resources I had. But indeed, I would have shared the whole experience with a co-founder. If the start-up journey is already difficult, it is much more so if you are doing it as a solo founder. It's really important to have someone else to share the responsibility and workload with and especially to be able to encourage each other in the ups and downs of the start-up rollercoaster.

Starting up is hard and sharing the experience with another person can make the path easier.

In a more detailed aspect, I would also have launched our Minimum Viable Product (MVP) way before we did. We waited 9 months and now I see how we could have had optimized the time to minimize the economical investment. One of the improvements I would implement if I could go back in time is adding to the team a marketing specialist in my market area, so I could have set a strategy right away and not begun from scratch.

## BrioAgro Tech

> **Pitch:** BrioAgro provides intelligence to the farmers of conditions that may threaten crops, to take proper action in a timely manner via mobile app.
> **Author/s:** José Luis Bustos (CEO), Antonio Manuel Santos (CTO), Fran González Guillén (COO).
> **Location:** Spain, Seville, Mairena del Alcor.

### *1st Question*

We started in the 'campiña' (countryside) of Seville, in Mairena del Alcor, thanks to a local initiative to promote entrepreneurship.

I did not feel any disadvantages, rather the opposite; I was feeling lucky that in my region there were such initiatives to help give that necessary push to start a project.

The differences regarding other ecosystems are, on the one hand, financing and, on the other, the ecosystem itself; the larger, more varied and transversal it is, the more entrepreneurship, creativity and growth of ideas and projects are encouraged.

I think the main problem of innovative start-ups is locating clients who use your products/services and the ecosystem that encourages that, both from companies and from public institutions; this will really help validate start-ups in local markets, to help them go out and scale.

### *2nd Question*

We adapted with little budget, a lot of desire and, especially, we went out to the street to validate the hypotheses of the work before dedicating more time and money.

We pivoted regarding our initial idea and when we found the focus, we went for it and presented ourselves to the first edition of the first agri-food accelerator in Europe, ORIZONT, and, when we entered, we went to another level, which we have maintained and exceeded.

We built a very small team of computer engineers and agronomists and we looked for ways to have minimum viable products as soon as possible to install our smart irrigation developments on farms and, at the same time, learn from each case, from each crop, climate and casuistry, with the CEO at the foot of each project, learning like a sponge about everything.

With products already validated by us, we initiated commercial action focusing on the largest companies, which value measurable results, crediting them with savings thanks to our solutions and, in turn, hoping to scale to the maximum number of farms managed by them.

### 3rd Question

What I would change would be to dedicate less time to the project and more to the sales. In other words, to put aside a few more ideas that seem to be useful and sell what clients already need, right now. And with money in the box, I would improve what is offered to clients by developing parts of those initial ideas.

Selling innovation is difficult and even more so in rural areas.

The main tips for rural areas are:

- Use and dominate the Internet, a window to the world, to work in rural areas and sell anywhere.
- Sell what they demand, not what you think they will demand.
- And learn everything, every time. If that knowledge cannot be transferred by your neighbours, it can be by those you know in other places thanks to the Internet.

## PigCHAMP

**Pitch:** We help professionals in the livestock sector (producers, veterinarians and managers) get more out of the data they generate, making more informed decisions that help them improve the efficiency and quality of production.

**Author/s:** Gema Montalvo (R&D and Projects Manager), Carlos Piñeiro (CEO), Jaime Rodríguez-Monsalve (Marketing Manager).

**Location:** Spain, Segovia.

### 1st Question

PigCHAMP was born from the need of a large pig producer to have its own R&D and innovation service. Our first headquarters were in Madrid, but we soon realized that we had to be close to our sector and we set up our office in the city of Segovia. Over time, we have seen that being in a small city has many advantages (proximity to our livestock clients, not losing contact with the farm sector, quality of life for our employees), but also a few disadvantages (distance to airports, frequent trips to Madrid for meetings with large clients, also Ministries and National Administrations, search for specialized personnel, etc.). Although these disadvantages would possibly be solved in a business hub, the balance of being in a small city has been very positive for us.

### 2nd Question

At the beginning, we had two main departments: the applied research department and the data management and analysis department. The first one mainly met the needs of the parent company, although we were, little by little, getting external customers, such as large pharmaceutical laboratories or manufacturers of feed additives. And the second one gave support for the correct operation of a farm management software used by the farmer partners of the parent company, all of them located in our province or in a nearby area. Our staff used to go from farm to farm installing or updating the software and training the farmers in computer matters. After the sudden bankruptcy of the parent company, we had to adapt to a new situation: if we wanted to survive, we had to offer our services to any client, wherever they were. Thanks to the efforts of our staff and after many trips, fairs, congresses, meetings and so on, we were able to expand nationally and internationally. The development of Information & Communication Technology (ICT) has been our great ally in all these years and it has become a fundamental pillar in our work strategy.

### 3rd Question

Your rural users are not like common users (don't follow exactly all the books on customer experience, user research . . .). You need to connect with them, because they are not so communicative and do not trust so easily, so focus on connecting with them and interact with them to find the real problems. After a while we developed some tools, such as 'performance challenge', where they need to act as an input supplier, farming advisor, farmer, buyer, driver and other stakeholder to understand how they see the world and each role.

## Kharty

**Pitch:** Kharty is an educational app that helps you learn with interactive images.

**Author/s:** Pablo Bernal (Founder and IT), Francisco Montiel (CEO), Guillermo Piñero (Graphic Designer), Manuel Pedrero (BD).
**Location:** Spain, Murcia, La Flota.

## *1st Question*

Kharty started in Murcia, which is one of the lesser known regions of Spain and is focused on agricultural production.

It emerged as an altruistic project to help a friend study civil service. We came up with the idea of representing the street map of our city with terms marked by dots in an interactive image.

Our big disadvantage was that we did not have enough resources to finance the project, nor nearby centres to help us grow.

The big differences with the rest of the business ecosystem in Spain is that in Murcia there are only a few places to start a start-up and there are not many seats. Our options were low and we were very limited by our professions.

When we developed the test for our friend, we realized the potential of the project and how much it could help other people.

So, we worked nights and weekends to be able to launch the project with little money and we travelled to visit and meet other start-ups in different regions to learn how they do it.

## *2nd Question*

Today Kharty is a reality. It is already an app that can be downloaded from anywhere in the world. But our first steps were difficult. Pablo, the founder, came up with the idea of gathering close friends with the necessary skills to be able to develop and launch the project. The most important thing was to know how to program and design.

Once we gathered the necessary team (Pablo, Guillermo, Manolo and Fran) we started drawing on paper what our new project would be. Soon after, we faced a big issue for our team: two of us got jobs abroad and had to move.

We learned to work as a team remotely with tools like Skype and at times when we could all be connected, that is, during nights and on weekends. For two years, we dedicated ourselves to researching, learning and studying in order to develop our app.

Finally, we managed to have our first prototype. When we launched it, we realized that our design was already outdated. Despite having a good idea, we had to focus on improving our image to attract people. Meanwhile, in our free time and holidays, we travelled to look for and meet companies that wanted to support or teach us. We toured fair after fair until we finally met our first client and it was the great Telefónica, thanks to which we are here today.

### 3rd Question

If we could go back in time, we would only change one big thing and that is to have bet more on our idea and to have dedicated ourselves to it full time. It is difficult for a team when it starts to have the self-confidence and enough resources to dive into the void. Now we see that it is not necessary to have big hubs or companies that help you to start, although they are necessary to help you grow.

You simply need passion, belief in yourself and willingness to launch your project and embark on this beautiful path.

## Alén Space

> **Pitch:** At Alén Space we design, build and operate small satellites to put our clients' businesses into orbit.
> **Author/s:** Guillermo Lamelas (CEO).
> **Location:** Spain, Pontevedra, Nigrán.

### 1st Question

We started in Galicia, northwest Spain. Even if the start-up ecosystem is smaller than in the big hubs, I would say that there is a strong technological entrepreneurial culture in Galicia. Therefore, we didn't find lack of willingness, knowledge or experience, but like in many other places, the challenge comes when you need access to funding. In this regard, institutional support programmes aiming at promoting entrepreneurship were key in our first steps (ViaGalicia and Ignicia Programmes).

Once incorporated, the main difficulty we faced was finding the right investors. It was not a matter of being out of the big hubs, it was a matter of being a company focused on hardware. Most acceleration programmes and tech investors are specialized in software-centred start-ups that require small investments to test their business model. When it comes to B2B, hardware and long sales cycles, finding the right support and investors becomes an incredibly big challenge in Spain.

Because our market is global, it doesn't make a big difference whether you are based in Nigrán, in London or in Kuala Lumpur. However, besides the already mentioned lack of specialized funding sources, differences come from access to talent and to R&D funding opportunities. In Galicia, we have access to a large pool of technological talent. Regarding R&D funding, even if there are regional and national programmes to support R&D, it is our competition that benefits from stronger government policies to promote the space sector in their home countries.

### 2nd Question

This is a rare animal. We are a spin-off of the University of Vigo. The team that had been leading the development of small satellites in Spain from 2007 decided to create a company to exploit the commercial potential of this kind of satellite.

With the support of the university and the Ignicia Programme (by Xunta de Galicia—Regional Government), the team and technology transfer to the new start-up was performed. New business profiles were also enroled to complement the technical ones. On this basis, we started to visit potential partners and clients. Recognizing the potential of our technology and expertise, those visits soon opened up exciting business development opportunities.

Being in a global niche market means that potential clients are difficult not only to visit but also to spot. So, we bet for an inbound marketing strategy and presence in the main congresses in the sector. From this point of view, we undoubtedly believe that it is the same bet we would have had to do if we had started in a big entrepreneurship hub.

However, we found our first clients through the contacts our technical team already had in the sector. Selling is closely related to building trust. In that sense, I suppose it is natural to have as early adopters those who already know you.

As for taking advantage of a global market and the need to travel, I must say that Galicia is less connected than hubs like Madrid or Barcelona, which means that any trip will take a little longer and will be a little more expensive. This is clearly a disadvantage, but we consider it fully offset by the fact that we are developing our business where we want to live—a place where the quality of life is excellent, which generates great potential to keep attracting great talent.

### 3rd Question

My first piece of advice is to start with commercial and business development activities as soon as possible. Urgency, in this regard, is a key factor. The sooner you start searching out your potential clients and start building trust-based links, the better. A good tip for B2B start-ups is to organize weekly trips to hubs where many potential clients and/or partners can be

found, trying to fill the agenda with meetings, letting those potential clients/
partners know about your company capabilities and offerings while grasp-
ing some relevant information about their challenges and pains.

A second piece of advice is to leverage the strengths of the area where
you are located. Quality of life may be a great source of happiness and,
therefore, loyalty for your current employees and a key asset to attract new
talent.

Third piece of advice: ask for support from your local/regional government. You have the potential to attract richness and create quality jobs and
this objective is probably totally aligned with your local government's goals.

# 9   USA

## Coordinator: Susan Giesecke

### Zero Grocery

**Pitch:** Zero Grocery provides a convenient, zero-waste grocery delivery service. Zero Grocery's mission is to remove single-use plastics from the food system so customers will receive groceries in reusable containers.
**Author/s:** Zuleyka Strasner (CEO and Entrepreneur).
**Location:** Oakland, California (San Francisco Bay).

#### 1st Question

Where did I start? In Berkeley, because there I was given the impetus, training, confidence and information needed to launch my start-up.

At first, I did feel that there were disadvantages compared to other start-ups that started in big cities, because I had thought about and matured the idea in my house, in my bedroom, in my small area of operation. But it is true that the Sutardja programme allows you to go to Berkeley, get to know the university, the environment, other entrepreneurs and, from there, make the leap.

In my opinion, the difference between the entrepreneurial ecosystem where I started and others is the attitude. In Berkeley, at the Sutardja, they make you feel that if your idea is good you can reach the goal, so if you have the desire and the necessary training, the environment, rural or not, doesn't matter. In fact, today our environment is much more rural than urban, although large supermarket chains, such as Whole Foods, already trust us.

Because, in fact, your idea (or, in this case, mine) could be carried out anywhere, all I had to do was to make the commercial network. Then, with technology, we have been able to achieve everything.

#### 2nd Question

I adapted to the environment with a combination of keys: (1) attention to my surroundings, to see what was happening, what my start-up needed;

(2) continuous learning, of what Sutardja taught me and what other class-mates gave me; and (3) knowing how to change the chip. My idea was good; in fact, it still is. And there are already several twin companies in the world. I don't know if mine was the first but in this part of California there wasn't one and I implemented it. And then it happened that Whole Foods got interested. And then it happened that Amazon bought Whole Foods and that's how the snowball got fat.

The first steps were simple: I had an idea, I asked for help and I went and trained. At the University of California Berkeley, I was welcomed with open arms and that's where I finished my training.

My first team was basically made up of trusted people who shared my principles, my desire to learn and my need to stay with the company. Then the first customers arrived, which were basically local. What's more, a large percentage of the customers today are local, but we have a battery of large customers who, although not many, are very powerful and give us solvency and profitability.

So, we combine both markets.

### 3rd Question

Well, actually . . . I think it would change little if I could go back in time. I mean, sure, knowing what I know now I could have done different things and made fewer mistakes, but those mistakes helped me know what I know today. So, I'm not sure if I would change much or not. What I would do again is get into an environment of training for entrepreneurs, whether Sutardja, or any other. Well, in the end, the partners are teaching, the teachers are teaching, the companies that tutor you are tutoring. And all this is necessary.

So, to sum up a little, as advice for entrepreneurs in rural areas I would say that:

1. Be aware of your environment.
2. Learn and train yourselves.
3. Be open to change and adaptation to the reality of your market.
4. Do not give up your local and rural character, because with the great variety of technologies that exist, many things can be done.

My company is 100% rural, located in the Bay area, with distribution and intermediation of products from agriculture and livestock. Something that, a priori, could have stayed there. But with computer technology we have been a profitable start-up. Counsel: let them follow that union and not give up on entrepreneurship.

# 10  Portugal

## Coordinator: Pedro Alvaro Pereira Correia

### Connecting Software

**Pitch:** We make any software developer a hero of integration in less than 3 hours for more than 400 business and industrial applications, with special attention to local and rural SMEs and micro-SMEs. The important value of our start-up is that we develop software based on blockchain technologies and database solutions, but always with a very local and rural focus.
**Author/s:** Thomas Berndorfer (CEO).
**Location:** Portugal, Madeira.

### 1st Question

I started at an initiation centre in Malacky, Slovakia. We chose that place, far from a big city, to have less competition and less fluctuation of people. Since we can afford to be in a rural environment, because we don't need our clients to come to our offices, we went for a village. Later, when we began to receive more orders and, above all, from other parts of Europe (yes, Europe!) and with the development and entrepreneurial team, we considered the possibility of looking for another location with the same characteristics. Rural, local, with good weather . . . and we looked in Spain and Portugal. Finally, Universidade da Madeira not only welcomed us in its entrepreneurship and accelerator programme, but the conditions offered to us in an environment like Funchal were unbeatable. In addition, we were able to access investors who, being local, supported us from the beginning.

Although before we started, we were considering starting our activity in a big city, because of the business traffic, finally, when we decided to change the course, we did not feel that there was less business capacity because our activity works perfectly in a rural context.

## 2nd Question

We gradually adapted to the environment. We started with two people in a start-up centre locally and then we started working on growing. Our goal has always been to grow in products, resources and benefits, but to stay with the good that the local offers us.

Being able to set up an office anywhere with Internet, we had little to adapt to; it was quite easy.

## 3rd Question

It would change very little.

The first mistake was that I hired cheap and unqualified people and this was a mistake; later I focused more on quality. You must hire talent and have the optimal resources, whether you are Google or a small, local company.

The local connections were pretty good from the beginning, which helped us grow; and the customers never cared about our physical address, because we have good online customer service.

## Press Power

> **Pitch:** PressPower is a media processing and information dump centre (clipping), as well as a centre of transcription of speeches, news and audiovisual communications for print media.
> **Author/s:** Francisco Freitas (Founder and CEO), Raquel Braga (COO).
> **Location:** Portugal, Madeira, Funchal.

## 1st Question

Our beginning was quite simple: a computer, our training and the desire to conquer the world. We also started with a service that, at the beginning, was not provided by any other competitor, which was based on a specific technology: we provided the market with a news service oriented to the needs and objective interests of very local companies, as part of the management of their information.

We provide our clients with the possibility of achieving total mobility of their news archive, filters and information crossing, receiving all their news with quality through a mobile application—a completely innovative, simple and effective application.

The differences with large companies are enormous: the networks, the physical and human resources are examples and, in that sense, we did see our capacity to compete reduced; however, both the local costs and the support from entities (public and private) made us succeed. And here we continue.

## *2nd Question*

The beginnings were complicated, because fighting giants is complicated. But we made up for it with lots of personal effort and personal networking.

Nevertheless, as we indicated, several organizations supported us and caused us to have solvency and helped us grow.

The fact of being in a rural environment and orienting our business to local organizations as our first clients (although, with growth, we already include national companies) did not, in fact, create much upheaval. Rather, it made it easier for us, even if the beginning was harder.

## *3rd Question*

Nothing. We did our best and Start-up Madeira was the biggest start-up Madeira centre. Thanks to them we are where we are now and the truth is that we have done well.

I don't think I would change anything. Rather, I think we should promote this very thing: more locally based companies supported by technology. Start-up Madeira does it and is achieving many things.

# 11 Latin America (Peru and Brazil)

*Coordinator: Patricia M. Farias Coelho*

*Special Thanks: Mónica Reyes*

## Agros

> **Pitch:** Bring digital and financial inclusion to family farmers in Latin America.
> **Author/s:** Robinson López (CEO), Hugo Piñarreta (COO).
> **Location:** Perú, Piura.

### 1st Question

We started working on solving a problem in family farming, so we started working in a city close to rural areas, which seemed natural, and using local connections to users and stakeholders helped us a lot to have a clear view about the problem we were facing. Nevertheless, we had a hard time when we needed to start testing solutions and building an Minimun Viable Product (MVP).

Usually, in cities far away from the capital, getting access to professionals in User Experience, Cloud Communication Platforms or Mobile Developers is not easy; and not many of them like the idea of travelling and working outside the capital (for UX, being in contact with farmers was critical). So that's why it took a long time for us to find our team members and start developing the product.

### 2nd Question

We found that there's a value that small towns have and big cities don't. You develop a close relationship with your environment and that is why we invaded the house of one of the founders (mine) and built a 'home' environment; everybody has lunch together as a family and this offers added value against other start-ups: 'bonding'! At the same time, every two weeks we had 'field missions' and sent team members to gather information from farmers and their fields to 'understand' who they were working for and how they lived and that helped us develop a purpose and love for the moonshot!

Our first customers arrived as soon as we identified the 'leader' of the farmers' community, because they had many contacts with stakeholders and that's how we got the first one. It's crucial to believe in the purpose of the company and the influence of the 'leader' (Don José).

### 3rd Question

Your rural users are not like common users (they don't exactly follow all the books on customer experience, user research, etc.).

You need to build with the users because they are not so communicative, and they don't trust so easily, so focus on developing with the users and interacting with the users to find the real problems. After a while we developed some tools, as 'acting challenges', where they need to act as an input supplier, farming advisor, farmer, buyer, driver and other stakeholders to understand how each role sees and understands the world.

## Ticsart

> **Pitch:** Ticsart is a platform that develops strategies to increase the adoption of technology by small craft businesses and gives them visibility throughout the world with our marketplace.
>
> **Author/s:** Monica Alexandra Chavez Llancay (CEO), Harold Huidobro Casas (CTO), Gabriela Farfan Enríquez (CMO), Ruth Ebely Llalla Cahuana (CFO).
>
> **Location:** Perú, Cusco.

### 1st Question

In Cusco, there is no ecosystem of start-ups, as it is a city of small family businesses dedicated to tourism, mainly focused on Machu Picchu as the centre of its economy. So, our resources and opportunities have always been limited, and even more so tthere was no support from the university, the government or large companies.

At first, we felt lost, because we were alone and far from any ecosystem, which made it take us longer than if we had an ecosystem. We had a constant battle to make them believe in us, because we were one of the first to want to innovate in an industry that has little support and visibility for being rural. However, that made us be more courageous and make the most of every opportunity that came our way.

Last year we decided to technify our knowledge and be part of the ecosystem in Peru, so we moved to Lima. We worked hard and, thus, we were recognized as the best e-commerce venture in Peru in 2019 by the Ecommerce Institute.

After a few months, we also managed to be part of the Leaders in Innovation Fellowship programme of the Royal Academy of Engineering and go to London. We strengthened ourselves to be part of the ecosystem, because we were able to learn from the experience of other entrepreneurs and articulate with others.

## 2nd Question

It was more difficult than we could imagine, being able to work with artisans with the barriers of language, age, tradition, reluctance towards technology and being used to their routines. We had to be very creative and flexible. I remember when we travelled to the first community with volunteers who helped us as models and we did the whole process of taking photos, editing, technical sheets and then uploading everything to the web. We were determined to put them online, so we could give them a digital window to improve their businesses. We knew that we could apply our superpower of technology to an industry like crafts; even today we have a long way to go and reach more families.

Peru is a country of small informal businesses, afraid of formality, because it is thought that you will have more problems than opportunities. Even so, when we formalized our project and presented it to Start-up Peru for seed capital, we won it, but these are opportunities that 80% of companies don't have a chance to get.

We are challenged to make the customer fall in love with the product through a photograph. This implies that we are aware of the entire value chain, not only on the web, but seeing that the artisans produce it, seeing the materials and going to their houses, which led us to meet them and know their needs, family stories and also their fraternal culture.

## 3rd Question

I would not change anything if I went back in time, as this is to help my family of artisans. Being an entrepreneur is always going to be difficult but doing it in rural areas has an additional difficulty, because you have to be aware of your clients and your beneficiaries, since giving them the best implies twice the work and also more satisfaction.

We learned a lot from our mistakes, because our hypotheses made us go back one step in the value chain. We went from the artisan businessman to the entrepreneur to the marketer until we reached the producer and we had to prove to whom we give more value.

Knowing that entrepreneurs in rural areas are around the world, what we need is to be able to connect to share our experiences and articulate ourselves.

The incredible thing about being an entrepreneur is that among entrepreneurs we always help each other and apply 'pay it forward'. So I can tell you that you are not alone; just work hard, learn a lot and we will meet soon.

It helped us have our WHY, 'empowering with technology', because we never abandon our essence as Ticsart and even if it is to teach the most basic of technology, it is a step on the road to digitalization.

## Evobooks

**Pitch:** We develop Interactive Digital Classrooms in 3D with a focus on improving the learning experience in and out of schools.
**Author/s:** Felipe Rezenade (CEO and Founder).
**Location:** Brazil, São Paulo.

### 1st Question

Well, we started, I guess, like everybody else, with an idea in a garage. We were several heads, each thinking along the same lines but about different things. I don't know, we started in 2011 with an idea, we matured it, we proposed a technology and it turned out that it didn't exist. And we patented it. And we were able to develop it.

We did feel that we were at a disadvantage. We came from different rural areas: Campinas, Joinville, or even from districts like Morumbi. You have to think that São Paulo is such a big city that many of its districts function as towns do in Europe.

And in this sense, we looked small. But we started and soon made the jump to São Paulo City. And there we did have, not only the take-off, but also the support of the government and many private educational entities.

### 2nd Question

Well, we studied our audience very well: publishers, schools, academies, parents, universities . . . and we approached them. At first timidly and then with the solvency that our products and our customers gave us. And the jump to the city of São Paulo was crucial.

We studied our clients well, we studied our economic possibilities well and we minimized as much as possible the risks that could come from Brazilian society.

But I must say that it didn't take much effort either because our product was good (as demonstrated) and adapted quickly.

At the beginning, it is true, we were humble and set too low a price in our economic plan. But we just had to adjust it and that was it.

### 3rd Question

Well, the truth is that I wouldn't know how to answer, because we have made mistakes . . . but we have been taught to grow and correct them. We've basically learned, so if I changed anything, I'd still screw up.

I could list all the mistakes I've made, but I can't answer that I would change them because they have been part of my training, of my master's degree in entrepreneurship, of my master's degree as a manager and salesman.

I wouldn't change anything. At least not for my company. I would change many things about the environment, of course, but it is not in my power.

# 12 United Kingdom

*Coordinator: Irene García Medina*

## Beira

**Pitch:** Sustainable slow luxury womenswear.
**Author/s:** Dr Antoinette Fionda-Douglas (Co-Founder), Flavio Forlani (Co-Founder).
**Location:** Scotland, Edinburgh, and Italy, Bergamo.

*1st Question*

Beira started as a joint venture between Dr Antoinette Fionda-Douglas and Flavio Forlani. We took a very lean approach to the start-up but also a slow, considered approach. It was a difficult process and involved a lot of self-motivation as we were not involved in a big hub at inception. However, 6 months after we launched, Antoinette was awarded a place in the Creative Bridge programme at Codebase in Edinburgh. This programme facilitated creativity, innovation, entrepreneurship and networking. It also allowed the founder to spend quality time with the business and not just be focused on the day to day.

*2nd Question*

The first steps were to create the brand concept, holistic brand identity and values, mission and vision.

Once we had a clear idea of those, we designed in reverse using a reverse resources method and relied on the waste we could purchase to drive the design process.

Once we had clarity on all these aspects, we spoke to lawyers, accountants and created the limited company and then started the production process. The team involves Antoinette and Flavio at the core, then the team at La Rocca, the manufacturer, to aid in the production process.

Customers were reached through a combination of strategies, firstly creating images to promote the collection on social media, networking, community groups, podcasts and other media. The brand and first collection were officially launched as part of Fashion Revolution Week in Scotland with a catwalk show.

There were numerous events including charity events and pop-up shops which all helped establish relationships with our first customers. We quickly discovered that events that allowed the customers to ascertain the quality and cut of the product led to increased sales.

*3rd Question*

I think I would have been involved in some facilitated programmes for start-ups earlier in the process. There is a lot of help available in Scotland and gaining access to this was not difficult; it just involved a lot of time and effort. Interestingly, the impact of the 2020 lockdown has led to more content being available online, which has been very helpful and allowed us to access more events and resources.

## Yellow Bird Digital

> **Pitch:** Our flagship product is a Customer Relationship Management (CRM) that allows small (very small) businesses, many of them agricultural and livestock, to sell from their mobile phones without the need for great knowledge and with the synergy that gives, for example, local information networks.
> **Author/s:** Nicola and Lindsay Erskine (Co-Founders).
> **Location:** Scotland, Edinburgh.

*1st Question*

We started with one hand in front and one hand behind. With a desktop computer in our room. And with a lot of desire to conquer the world!

When I started my business, I was very keen to do as much networking as possible and meet new business contacts, as I found that was what helped me through and got my name out there, so I could begin to build my reputation.

We had an idea, raised it with some acquaintances and got some feedback. Then we tried (without much success) to sell our product, but an acquaintance told us that we had to give the sensation of a company with more solvency. And so, we did.

We started to sell our idea of how to promote local brands and local products because we started in our parents' house, in a village outside Edinburgh.

And some companies started to hire us, but with basic marketing services. And then we had the idea to bring the digital world closer to the rural world, which was not so clear. And we saw the light of the germ of what our CRM would later be, and we won a prize for start-ups in the region and what led us to Glasgow, which is the business capital (the cultural one is Edinburgh).

## 2nd Question

If you don't adapt, you die. You have to survive and sometimes grow. We adapted to the urban public of Glasgow, as we came from a rural context which, although a priori I would say is more difficult, for us was easier. And the jump to Glasgow . . . cost us. But we learned to get into the heads of the local Glasgow micro-businesses while continuing with our small businesses that helped us be born.

We simply adapted. It's as if you only have bananas to eat and you don't like them, so either you eat them, or you die. Well, we were the same: there were things that we did not like, but we learned to value them; and those that we did like, we exploited, as in a SWOT matrix (Strengths, Weaknesses, Opportunities and Threats).

## 3rd Question

Probably saying yes to more opportunities, getting on more projects, covering more, because at the beginning we were naïve and said no to projects that we could cover but that scared us—vertigo.

I think we should tell entrepreneurs that they should throw themselves into projects and that if they make mistakes or don't get there, nothing happens: you learn from it and that's it.

I think that, if I could, I would change that attitude of being indecisive at the beginning and say yes to more projects.

# Contributors

## Editors

### Gloria Jiménez-Marín

PhD in Communication. She has a degree in Journalism and a degree in Advertising and Public Relations from the University of Seville (Spain). She is a senior lecturer at the Faculty of Communication at the same university, and collaborates at the Universitat Oberta de Catalunya. She has been a lecturer at University of Wales (UK) and postdoc at University of California Berkeley (USA) and Glasgow Caledonian University (UK). She is the editor of *International Review of Communication and Marketing Mix*, a member of the Spanish Advertising Academy, and developer of *Anagrama—Communication & Marketing*.

### Alejandro López Rodríguez

Entrepreneur. A professional in the travel industry, and an international trade expert for more than 10 years, his interests turned from languages and logistics to data science, after he was a scholarship holder in Silicon Valley. As a data scientist, he has developed successful products that combine tourism and statistics.

### Miguel Torres García

PhD in Engineering at the School of Higher Technical Engineering from the University of Seville, Spain. He has been the Director of Knowledge Transfer and Entrepreneurship since 2015 and is the driving force behind numerous initiatives based on the knowledge generated at the University of Seville for society.

### José Guadix Martín

Professor of Business Organization and Vice-Rector of Technology Transfer at the University of Seville (Spain). He has been Director of the Secretariat of Knowledge Transfer and Entrepreneurship at the same university and Deputy General Director of the US Research Foundation (FIUS), as well as Coordinator of the MP Chair at the University of

Seville and member of the Board of Directors of the Association for the Development of Organizational Engineering (ADINGOR).

In his research profile, his participation in numerous projects of the National Plan for R&D&I stands out; he has been Principal Researcher in several technology transfer projects financed in competitiveness by public entities and has directed research contracts with different companies. He is also the inventor of four patents with PCT extension licensed to private companies. His areas of interest in research are transport, project management and occupational risk prevention.

## Contributors

### Óscar Carreras Sandoval

A Spanish Linguistics graduate from the University of Zaragoza (Spain) with wide knowledge of new technologies resulting from an additional certificate in Advanced Computing. Currently Óscar works for Expedia as Director of SEO Global Product Marketing.

### José L. Córdoba Leiva

Director of Marbella's Andalucía Lab Tourist Innovation Centre, a tourism entrepreneurship hub where both start-ups and traditional tourist companies obtain support and education about new trends and technologies.

### Pedro Alvaro Pereira Correia

PhD in Marketing and Management and Marketing Professor at the graduate and master's levels, thesis supervisor and PhD and Master jury member at the Universidade da Madeira (Portugal). As a professional he has worked, among others, as marketing director, management consultant, project manager (Portuguese Chamber of Commerce, Portuguese Business Association, BICs, SGS, etc.) and External Senior Expert for European Structural and Investment Funds.

### Javier Domingo Morales

Lawyer, mentor and Business Development Specialist. He is involved in entrepreneurship initiatives developed by several Andalusian universities to teach their students in the subject of innovation.

### Marta Domínguez de la Concha-Castañeda

Senior Lecturer at the University of Seville (Spain) in the Department of Business Administration and Marketing and Market Research (Marketing); PhD in Economic and Business Sciences. She is linked to the area of entrepreneurship at the University of Seville.

### Rodrigo Elías Zambrano

PhD in Communication, degree in Audiovisual Communication, Master's in AV Business Management, Master's in AV Communication and

Education. He has been a lecturer at several Spanish universities, having been a scholarship holder at the Sutardja Center for Entrepreneurship and Technology at the University of California Berkeley, and at Glasgow Caledonian University. He is a developer of *A Foco Productions*. He is lecturer in University of Seville, Spain.

**Patricia M. Farias Coelho**

PhD in Communication and Semiotics from the Pontifical Catholic University of São Paulo, Brazil (2010), Post-Doctorate from the Post-Graduate Programme in Intelligence Technologies and Digital Design at Pontifical Catholic University of São Paulo, Post-Doctorate in Digital Communication from the University of Murcia (Spain), Post-Doctorate in Digital Communication from the Universitat Autonoma de Barcelona (Spain), Postdoctoral in the Education and Curriculum Programme and Postdoctoral in Communication and Consumption at the University of Seville (Spain).

**Irene García Medina**

Lecturer in Marketing at Glasgow Caledonian University (Glasgow, UK). She has a PhD in Marketing (University of Sophia—Antipolis, France). She has previous experience at the University of Madeira (Portugal), at the University of Vic (Spain) and at the University Pompeu Fabra (Spain). She has published numerous articles and books in the field of marketing.

**Susan Giesecke**

Director of Global Engagement, responsible for establishing partnerships with universities and international organizations interested in collaborating with the Sutardja Center for Entrepreneurship and Technology (SCET) at the University of California Berkeley (USA). Previously, she was Director of International Protocol in the Global Engagement Office (GEO) on the Berkeley campus.

**María del Mar González-Zamora**

PhD in Business Administration and Management from the University of Seville (Spain); University Lecturer in the Department of Financial Economics and Operations Management (University of Seville). Between February 2015 and July 2019 she was Vice-Dean of Business Relations and Entrepreneurship at the Faculty of Economic and Business Sciences and, since January 2018, Director of the Andalusia Emprende Chair at the University of Seville.

**Patricia Hernanz Falcón**

PhD in Biochemistry and Molecular Biology from Autónoma University of Madrid (National Center of Biotechnology), Spain, Post-Doctorate at the London Research Institute (Cancer Research UK). She specializes in Digital Products (Boston University, USA) and Agile methodologies (Certified Scrum Product Owner by Scrum Alliance; Certified SAFe 5 Agilist by Scaled Agile, Inc.). She successfully ran her own company for 6 years with Expedia as one of her main clients and currently works for HSBC, leading the retail bank accessibility and digital design governance programmes across all digital products and platforms, markets and channels.

**Tom Horsey**

Investor and 'business angel', founder of the Startup Labs accelerator. Entrepreneur and co-founder and CMO at Mox.

**Félix Jiménez-Naharro**

University Lecturer in the knowledge area of Financial Economics and Accounting. He has a PhD in Business Administration and a Master's in Entrepreneurship, Search for Financing and Business Valuation at the University of Seville.

**Víctor López Pérez**

Lawyer specializing in technology and founder of LBO Abogados, where he provides legal advice to entrepreneurs and start-ups.

**Patricia López Trabajo**

Leads the MYHIXEL project. Born in Seville, Spain, she has extensive experience in diverse sectors, among them tourism and the intimate products industry. In fact, after working for a leading brand in this field, she became aware of the lack of products for improving male sexual wellbeing. Therefore, she embarked on the adventure of founding MYHIXEL.

**Ignacio Morales Conde**

Efficient and reliable economist. He enjoys sharing all he has learnt in his 25-year professional career with start-ups and, therefore, put in practice expertise, business vision, forward thinking and passion to help them grow faster and more focused. He is good at finding best practices worldwide that could be implemented elsewhere and is very enthusiastic to get involved in projects that help complex organizations become digital.

**Álvaro Pareja Domínguez**

Engineer and mentor specialist in customer development strategies and lean start-ups. Álvaro provides advice to start-ups and entrepreneurs in Andalucía Open Future.

**Ricardo San Martín**

PhD in Biotechnology from the Imperial College of London (UK). He is an inventor and entrepreneur in chemical and biological sciences,

Professor of Entrepreneurship and Innovation, Research Director and Co-Founder of the Alt. Meat Program at the Sutardja Center for Entrepreneurship and Technology (SCET) at the University of California Berkeley (USA) and Innovation Director of Desert King International in San Diego, California (USA). Now he is a professor at University of California Berkeley.

**Emilio Solís Bueno**

Biologist and entrepreneur. Emilio has been designing and managing entrepreneurial programs for universities for more than 5 years with his Ideas Factory initiative, where hundreds of students have had their first contact with business innovation.

# Index

accelerator(s) 6–8, 52, 58, 67
adapt 3, 9, 16, 33, 35–36, 41, 49, 52–54, 57–58, 60, 65–66, 68, 73, 77
advertising x, 22–23
agile 32, 35–36, 41

business angel 13, 57

code/coding 30–32, 33, 36, 52
communication x, 17, 19–23, 29, 38, 42, 46–47, 68
community(ies) ix, xi, xiv, 3–5, 7, 71–72, 76
competitivity 16, 18, 20–22, 24–26, 36, 41, 63, 67
connection(s) xii, 4–5, 20, 22, 32, 54, 68, 70
consumer(s) 16–23
cooperation 5, 13, 27
cost 3, 5, 11–12, 18–19, 25–29, 34, 44, 53, 68, 77
creative/creativity ix, x, 7, 33, 35, 58, 72, 75
crowdfunding 13–14
customers 6, 15–26, 28, 32, 36–38, 43, 49, 52–54, 56, 60, 65–66, 68, 71–73, 76

development xiii, 3–6, 31, 33–37, 39, 55, 59–60, 63, 67
DIY (do it yourself) 33

economy ix, 5, 71
efficiency 59
enterprise(s) 5, 9

environment xi, xiv, 4–9, 17, 20–21, 25, 27–29, 36, 47, 49, 51, 54, 56–57, 65–70, 74

failure 10–11, 23, 34, 36, 38–39, 45, 47
feedback 36, 76
financing 5, 9–14, 33, 37, 40, 58
founding xiii, 57

growth ix, 6, 12, 16–17, 57–58, 69

incubation 6
incubator(s) 6–8
innovation x, xiii–xiv, 3, 10, 13, 59, 75
investor(s) 5–7, 12–14, 15n2, 21, 37, 40–43, 57, 62, 67

Kickstarter 57
Kotler, Philip 17–18

landing page 33
leader(s) ix, 7, 14, 36–38, 47, 71–72
lean start-up 36
learning x, 6–7, 35, 37, 47, 52, 59, 61, 66, 73

marketing 3, 17–21, 25–26, 28, 37, 52, 58, 63, 77
mentor(s) 6–7, 41, 51
methodology 6–7, 36, 38
mistake(s) 10, 26, 35, 39, 41–42, 46, 52, 66, 68, 72, 74, 77

network ix, xiii, 5–7, 13, 22–23, 44, 46, 52, 56, 65, 68–69, 75–76

operation(s) 5, 14, 21, 24–27, 60, 65
opportunity(ies) x, xi–xiv, 3, 6–7, 9, 31,
    44–46, 51, 55, 57, 62–63, 71–72, 77

patent xiii, 42, 73
platform ix, xiv, 14, 22, 31, 34, 57, 71
price 12, 17–21, 26, 28, 35, 73
problem x, xiii, 10, 32–33, 38, 40, 42,
    45, 55, 58, 60, 70–72
product xiv, 16–22, 24–28, 30–32,
    35–36, 39–40, 43–45, 52–53, 56, 58,
    70, 72–73, 76
profitability 12–13, 17, 26, 66
project x, 3, 7, 11–15, 17, 20, 22, 24,
    31–32, 36, 39–43, 45–46, 52–59,
    61–62, 72
public relations 7, 22

reputation 22, 76
resource 10, 12–13, 25, 27–28, 34,
    36–37, 40, 42, 51, 53–54, 57, 61–62,
    68, 71, 75–76

salary 15, 18, 35
service(s) 5–6, 16–28, 30, 39–42,
    58–61, 65, 68, 77
Silicon Valley xii, 5, 32, 51
skills x, 4–5, 13, 29, 36, 61

small business(es) ix, 76, 77
software 36, 60, 62, 67
solution(s) x, xiii–xiv, 10, 33, 36, 40,
    52, 56, 59, 67, 70
stakeholders 6, 60, 70–71
strategy 7, 21, 25–26, 36, 44–45, 58,
    60, 63
successful 15, 21, 26, 36, 41, 43, 56
SWOT (Strengths, Weaknesses,
    Opportunities and Threats) 77
synergie(s) xiv, 76

team xiv, 6–8, 12, 14, 25–26, 29, 31,
    33–41, 47, 52, 56–59, 61–63, 66–67,
    70, 75
technology(ies) x, xiii–xv, 4, 6, 9,
    13–14, 19, 22, 28, 30–32, 34–37,
    44–45, 51, 56, 60, 62–63, 65–69,
    71–73
third party(ies) 34, 41
transfer xii, 6, 29, 59, 63

validation 33
value 5–7, 10, 12, 16, 18–19, 22, 28,
    41, 45–46, 59, 67, 70, 72, 75, 77
village x–xi, xiii, 51, 56, 67, 76

WordPress 32–33

Printed in the United States
by Baker & Taylor Publisher Services